Praise for *The Angst of Adolescence* and Sara Villanueva, PhD

"Villanueva, a developmental psych. versational style in this helpful paren from her own experiences as a mother ing two teens, as well as up-to-date in. on brain development. Villanueva reminds readers that risky behaviors by teens reflect the fact that their brains are not yet fully developed. She also warns against 'drawing a line in the sand' as teens are likely to respond to 'forbidden fruits' with rebellion. With its encouraging tone, Villanueva's friendly primer will help parents learn to appreciate, enjoy, and accept their teens as they are, while patiently negotiating the challenges and changes inherent in adolescence."

—*Publishers Weekly*

"With humor and great warmth, Sara Villanueva tackles issues that can seem unsettling or bewildering to most parents. Her voice is reassuring, and by the end of the book you know you're not only up for the challenge of parenting a teen, but that you're not in it alone."

—Ami Albernaz, contributor to the *Boston Globe*

"While reading *The Angst of Adolescence*, I loved Sara's conversational voice, assurance, examples, information, and humor. I can't imagine any parent of a teen who wouldn't enjoy and profit from this mix of professional and personal insight."

—Carl Pickhardt, PhD, author of the blog and book, *Surviving Your Child's Adolescence*

"Sara Villanueva does a masterful job of balancing the sound advice of an experienced parent with the scientific literature of adolescent development and parenting. She strikes a tone that is both authoritative and completely conversational. I feel better equipped to tackle my son's upcoming transition into adolescence and wish this kind of parenting *instruction manual* were available sooner."
—Russell Frohardt, professor of psychology and behavioral neuroscience, St. Edward's University

"Sara Villanueva brings to light what so many parents of teens are feeling. By providing humorous anecdotes mixed with sound, research-based advice, all delivered in a relaxed and relatable style, she informs and reassures parents of the wonderful world of adolescence and how they can learn to laugh about it."
—Vicki Hoefle, author of *The Straight Talk on Parenting* and the best-selling *Duct Tape Parenting*

"*The Angst of Adolescence* will help every parent understand how to go through this difficult stage without losing their mind. According to Sara Villanueva, you could even have some fun along the way!"
—Jennifer Kerzil, PhD, associate professor of psychology, Université Catholique de l'Ouest, Angers, France

"Such a remarkable and much needed book! Dr. Villanueva's voice and personal stories, combined with her professional expertise, set the tone and made me laugh out loud! As a dean of students at a liberal arts university, and as a parent of a sixteen-year-old, the wisdom shared in this book is 'just in time' and speaks to the tumultuous times of transition that our teens experience and that we, as parents, encounter too. Her insight is smart, authentic, and extremely hopeful!"
—Lisa L. Kirkpatrick, PhD, associate vice president for student affairs/dean of students, St. Edward's University

THE ANGST OF ADOLESCENCE

THE ANGST OF ADOLESCENCE

HOW TO PARENT YOUR TEEN

(and live to laugh about it)

Sara Villanueva, PhD

bibliomotion inc.

First published by Bibliomotion, Inc.
39 Harvard Street
Brookline, MA 02445
Tel: 617-934-2427
www.bibliomotion.com

Printed in the United States of America

Library of Congress Cataloging-in-Publication Data

Villanueva, Sara.
    The angst of adolescence : how to parent your teen and live to laugh about it / Sara Villanueva. — First Edition.
        pages cm
    Summary: "The Angst of Adolescence promises to deliver trustworthy resource for parents of teens who are searching for answers and guidance about how to maneuver their way through this tricky developmental period. Dr. Sara Villanueva, a prominent psychologist specializing in the adolescent years, shares relevant research findings so that parents can be informed of the facts"— Provided by publisher.
    ISBN 978-1-62956-076-2 (paperback) — ISBN 978-1-62956-077-9 (ebook) — ISBN 978-1-62956-078-6 (enhanced ebook)
    1. Parent and teenager. 2. Adolescence. 3. Parenting. I. Title.
    HQ799.15.V55 2015
    306.874—dc23
                            2015014519

To the people who fill my days with absolute madness and insanity, set my hair on fire, and worry me incessantly, yet always fill me with immense joy, pride, the greatest sense of inspiration and purpose ... my children.

For Susan, Thomas, Sophia, & Gabriel

I am truly blessed to be your Mother.

CONTENTS

Contents

INTRODUCTION

Ah, the teen years: the time when your child *always* has to have the last word; when you observe that she is in constant angst, and, of course, when you regularly get the classic eye rolling with major attitude. You love your child more than anything, I know. But something's different, right? Parents often wonder, "What happened to my sweet little boy who loved to snuggle?" or, "What happened to my affectionate little girl who let me brush her hair and asked to brush mine?"

Around the time your child begins the second decade of life, things start to change in a fairly dramatic way. She is entering the developmental period that has been referred to with terms like "Storm and Stress" and "the Terrible Teens." Adolescence is a time of important transition for both child and parents. Some telltale signs that your child is transitioning from childhood to adulthood include: pubertal development, demonstrated by obvious physical and biological changes; cognitive development, shown by teens starting to think differently and beginning to challenge the way others think and act; and social development, demonstrated by teens' desire to make decisions about who they spend their time with and how they want to define themselves. My goal in writing this book is to help parents navigate some of the issues that come up during this exciting and sometimes difficult time. Parenting is hard, and parenting teens is even harder.

So, why not band together and share information that helps us all stay informed and maybe even helps each of us find some relief in knowing there are others out there experiencing fallout from the infamous teenage angst. Here are some of the questions I'll provide answers for in the chapters of this book:

- Why do my teen and I argue so much? How do I lessen the conflict, and how do we stay close? Does she even like me anymore?
- Why does my teen want to be with his friends all the time? Does he not love us anymore?
- My daughter *thinks* she's in love. How does she even know what love is?
- The "S" word: I'm not sure, but I think my son is having SEX. This scares me to death. What if he gets an STD? Or worse, what if he makes me a grandparent? How can I deal with this?
- I know it's normal to be curious about alcohol and drugs, but how do I manage this without pushing too far?
- Letting go: my son is going off to college and I'm feeling so sad. I don't want to be one of those overreacting moms, but I'm an emotional mess!

Please note that, although I am a developmental psychologist by training and have extensive experience in researching, teaching, and writing about adolescent development and parenting, much of the writing in this book comes from my perspective as a *parent*. Although I interject information based on current research, my goal is to relate to other parents of teens and shed some light on issues we all struggle with. In reading *The Angst of Adolescence*, I hope you can relate, learn, and enjoy!

1

Oh, How the Mighty May Fall

Understanding the Massive Changes Occurring in Your Family

When my daughter Sophia was a little girl, she used to look up at me with those big, beautiful blue eyes and say, "Mommy, you are *sooooo* smart…you know everything!" And I would smile and agree. She used to follow me around constantly, asking question after question about anything, about everything. All her questions began exactly the same way: "…And Mom, why can fish breathe under water and we can't?"; "…and Mom, how does candy make your teeth fall out?"; "…and Mom, why does Thomas have a penis and I don't?" I would take each question as an opportunity to impart my lifelong wisdom to my daughter, to both satisfy the human-sponge tendencies in her and to make sure that I did my part in creating the well-informed, responsible, thinking individual she would become. This, I felt, was my contribution to the future, to society, to the world.

Sophia didn't care about pedigrees or how many years I had gone to college. She never considered that I had numerous years of life experience and had made many (and I do mean many) mistakes in my life. All she knew at that time was that I had answers to her multitude of questions, which she launched like the steady pelt of shooting stars in the Leonids. I felt like Wonder Woman, with indestructible, bulletproof bracelets that absorbed the impact of incoming questions and shot back answers that were wise beyond even my years. Secret confession: there were times when parenting my young children was pretty darn good for my ego. My child was right: I *am* soooo smart, and I *do* know everything! There were other times, however, when I would say to Sophia and her three siblings, "Alright, no one is allowed to say the word 'Mom' again for at least one hour!" These were times that, as fellow parents, I'm sure you can relate to. At these times I felt overwhelmed, uncertain, and on more than one occasion, felt as though I was at the end of my rapidly fraying rope.

No matter what the age of your child, being a parent can be a tough job. In fact, I have found the parenting experience to be a conundrum of sorts. One minute you may feel as though you are on top of the parenting universe, responsibly and brilliantly creating a person you think will be the next Nobel Peace Prize winner. And the very next minute, you may feel a tsunami-sized wave of doubt and insecurity after taking a moment to assess your child-rearing abilities and the potential disaster you could cause with one parental misstep. So...much...pressure!

Nowhere in the instruction manual (yeah, right) did it say that parenting would be easy. It is a tireless job that often fills you with self-doubt and angst about whether you're doing a good enough job at the monumental task of raising another human being. As my mother says, "Parenting is not for cowards," and she's absolutely right. After all, it would be easier to let the kid sit in front of the TV for a few hours when we're so exhausted we can barely get out of bed. And rather than putting forth the effort involved in dutiful and conscientious parenting, it would be loads easier to simply let our teens do whatever it is they want, with no supervision and no worries! But, I get the feeling that I'm preaching to the choir here, because if you are reading this book, then you are invested; you care; you're willing to do the work. But the point is that when my children were young, I was on a colossal, golden pedestal. I was, in fact, *the* smartest, *the* coolest, *the* most beautiful woman on the planet, and that felt damn good.

What I didn't anticipate is just how far I would fall if that pedestal ever toppled over. And it did, of course. As my daughter got older, and certainly as she entered into the abyss we call adolescence, she started seeking answers elsewhere: her friends, her phone, Google, Twitter. It reminds me of the famous Mark Twain quote: "When I was a boy of fourteen, my father was so ignorant I could hardly stand to have the old man around. But when I got to be twenty-one, I was astonished at how much the old man had learned in seven years." In what seemed to me to be no time at all, I went from being the smartest mom in the history of motherhood to regularly hearing comments like, "Uh! Mom, you just don't get it…" and, "Mom, don't worry about it…you won't understand." Both, of course, accompanied by the classic and always appreciated rolling of the eyes that teens seem to have perfected over the years.

At the risk of making a huge understatement, let me say that parenting during the teen years is not at all great for your ego. Even with a bachelors, masters, and PhD in psychology, I, like Twain's old man, apparently lost some serious IQ points along my children's developmental path. What gives? I'm still the same person.

Still the same woman who works hard at being a well-respected academic, is committed to her family, and adores her children. If anything, I've become even smarter, with more life experiences under my belt. But the truth is, as children reach their teen years, their perspectives change and it's not in our favor . . . sorry, parents! In the eyes of my teenage daughter, I, a live, breathing, human being with an actual brain, have been replaced by a smartphone. Yes, that's it. A smart *person* has been replaced by a smart*phone*. This, my fellow parents, is a sad but true statement. So long to being the smartest person alive . . . for now.

When I say that I've been replaced by a phone, I don't necessarily mean the technology itself, although phones these days *can* be pretty darn entertaining. I, myself, have guilty pleasures like games and social networking sites that I check on a fairly regular basis. I'm talking about the way teens communicate using them: they text, they tweet, they Snapchat, they Instagram, they "talk" *at* people, not *with* them. At the risk of sounding a hundred years old, I'd say that teens today would essentially never look up from their screen were it not for life-sustaining necessities like eating and sleeping. I mean, really, who needs to have a face-to-face conversation with a person in front of you, especially your mother, when you've got five other conversations happening on your phone? (All of which are monumentally more interesting and relevant to you when you are fifteen.)

Back to the sad reality that I'm not the genius mom I used to be to my daughter. There are actual, scientifically proven reasons for this seismic relational shift between parents and their teenage children. In addition to the technological wrench that's thrown into the communication mix when children have smartphones, teenagers begin to experience some major changes within themselves. In fact, it is these shifts that are at the core of what it *is* to be a teen. The developmental period of adolescence is all about major transitions, and these transitions happen in three distinct domains: biological (puberty!), cognitive (attitude!), and social (friends!).

The Shifting Teen Landscape

You may have noticed some of these transformations in your own children, as they morph before your very eyes. First, the child goes through puberty, and this not only creates major fluctuations in hormonal levels (which has been shown to impact mood...shocker, right?), it also does something that parents have been dreading since the first time their little girl put on that cute, size 2T polka-dot bikini when she was a toddler. You remember taking those pictures of her with the chunky little thighs that rubbed together and the belly that just wouldn't quit. Now, your postpubertal baby girl looks like a total hottie, in a bikini that's not much bigger than the one she wore when she was two! She is now looking older, acting older, and wants to be treated like she's older. I'll talk more about puberty and all the wondrous and amazingly scary stuff that comes with it in chapter 4.

Second, children's thinking gets better and more refined as they reach adolescence. Remember, this is a good thing. I'm not talking about their brains getting bigger, because we know that by the time your child is six, his brain is already 95 percent of its adult size. What I mean is that teens' actual *thinking* is much more mature, and the processes involved in thought are significantly more efficient by the time kids go through adolescence. Our teens begin to think about their own thinking processes (called

5

metacognition) as well as *your* thinking process (called defiance). This is where it gets dangerous. No longer does your teen accept your answers as undeniable fact. You fell from that pedestal a while ago, you recall. Now, she questions everything. Everything. This is a major cognitive developmental accomplishment for teens, but for you as a parent, it means a time of constant doubt, speculation, and bickering because your child now challenges everything that comes out of your mouth. These are the times that you resort to phrases you swore you would never say: "Because I *said so*, that's why!" or "Because I'm *your mother*, that's why!" or "Because I'm *the adult*, that's why!" These are also the times you ask yourself, what happened to the days when my sweet little girl used to think I was *soooo* smart? Sigh. Because I know that many of you, as parents of teens, are desperately seeking answers to these questions, I will go into much more detail about the changes in your child's cognition in chapter 2 and address parent–adolescent conflict in chapter 3.

And, of course, we dare not forget about your teen's social world. It shouldn't come as much of a surprise when, instead of wanting to spend time with her parents or her family, your teen would now much rather spend time with friends, or even alone. This is typical of adolescents. You remember the feeling, don't you? Sitting through a dreaded, obligatory family dinner, or even worse, the torturous "quality time" with parents and their friends *and* their friends' kids (with whom you were supposed to all-of-a-sudden be best friends). All we could do, as teens, was count the seconds until it would all be over and we could go hang out with real people—our friends. The teenage years are when we all begin our quest for freedom. Teens' social interactions—hanging out with friends, noticing cute boys or girls, and yes, even spending obscene amounts of time on the latest popular social networking sites—become numero uno when it comes to social priorities.

This shift in social needs is not an indication that your child no longer loves you or the family (despite clear evidence to the contrary), because teens really do love and appreciate their parents in their own way. But spending time with friends, doing whatever it is that goes on in that underground, Illuminati-type society that adults are not privy to, is what they need to do right now. "Need?" you ask? Yes, need. This is where psychosocial development occurs. They begin to figure out who they are, who they want to be, how they want to be seen by others, who likes them and who doesn't, and who accepts them and who doesn't, all in the context of their own social arena. This is where they also learn about social roles (that is, how to be a good friend or a good romantic partner) as well as social rules and norms (what's allowed and what's not). Chapters 5, 6, and 7 all tackle different parts of the teenage social world, including social groups in school, peer pressure, friendships, romantic relationships and love, and (take a deep breath) the "S" word...adolescent sexuality. Despite the cringe factor inherent in some of these topics, we, as parents of teens, can benefit from open discussions on these issues, so we can make sense of the monumental changes occurring in our teens' lives.

Transformations at Home

Just as teens navigate a series of difficult changes and transitions, so does the family. As I mention the word "family," many different images may come to mind. In today's world, families come in all shapes, sizes, and varieties, and this is a beautiful thing. So, when I talk about the changes that families go through during the turbulent teen years, I'm referring not only to what many people think of as the "traditional family"—mom, dad, two-point-three kids, a dog, and a mortgage, although this family is certainly included—I'm also thinking of single parents, gay and lesbian couples, grandparents raising grandchildren, and many other variations on the family theme. The one common denominator these families share: they all experience the perilous joys of raising a teen. Of course, in addition to the various joys and challenges involved with so-called "nontraditional" settings, families may also differ in cultural and/or religious attitudes and belief systems, which presents yet another layer of depth to already multifaceted family dynamics. But those discussions are for another time. For now, we'll consider the overall experiences that many families, in various contexts, share when it comes to having a teen at home.

If you have a newly minted teenager in your house, you have likely come to the realization that things are just not the same. You can't quite put your finger on it (well, maybe you can), but something has changed. There has been some strange shift and everything and every*one* in your home seems just a little *off.* If you are the parent of an older teen, you are already well versed in this uneasy feeling but still may not be able to explain it, so I ask you to read on. As our children reach adolescence, relationships within the family undergo serious transformations.

Particularly as we reflect on the parent–child relationship, we see that as adolescents get older, they begin to play a more forceful role in the family. Typically, we notice a shift away from the asymmetrical relationship that kids had with parents, whereby little Johnny would do exactly what Mommy or Daddy said to do;

instead, there is movement toward a more equal relationship with parents, where teens voice their opinions and concerns and play an active role in making decisions. Because we have been accustomed to being the "grown-ups" who, by necessity, make daily decisions for the family (big and small), often without consulting our children, the fact that our teens want to chime in on everything from what we eat for dinner to what car we buy to where we go on vacation throws the entire family system out of balance. Whether we like it or not, because of their own cognitive development, teens come to recognize that they have a voice, one based on their *own* thoughts and opinions; they also realize that, in the interest of fairness and relational justice (again, with the cognitive development!), this voice should be heard and counted within the family. Because these changes in the family dynamic are happening so quickly, at least from our perspective, they seem to catch parents off guard, and our deer-in-the-headlights reaction is often an exasperated and sometimes frustrated, "What is happening?!"

In addition to suddenly becoming extremely vocal and free with his opinion, our teen has also become somewhat distant or aloof, a stark comparison to the warm, loving, snuggly kid who, just yesterday (okay, it *seems* like just yesterday), loved to give us hundreds of kisses and begged us to read one more story. Another hallmark of adolescence is physical and emotional distancing; at least on the surface, the closeness you once shared with your child seems like a faint memory. In reality, of course, the feelings of love and commitment are still there, they're just hidden under the new exterior that cognitive and physical maturity bring. This physical and emotional distancing, along with the fact that your teen is looking and sounding older (notice I did not say *mature*) can lead to increased daily conflict in your household…another dramatic shift. What all of this means is that, because your child's role within the family is changing, yours must too. Many parents see this as a loss of power, and the resulting family dynamic becomes centered around parents' power struggles with their teen. But I propose that we take a different perspective. Consider that, by becoming a bit distant both emotionally and physically, by (continually) interjecting her thoughts and opinions in family matters, and by questioning every decision or judgment you make as a parent, your teen is simply doing her job. To be clear, I am not suggesting that teens should be allowed carte blanche behavior, where they are allowed to overextend their new freedoms at the cost of others; of course, there must still be rules, boundaries, and common courtesy and respect. But we parents should understand that these shifts, both within the child and within the family as a whole, are part of the normal developmental process.

Because I am in the midst of raising teens myself, I am well aware of the fact that it is not easy to take the perspective that kids' constant questioning is positive. In fact, despite all the formal training that led to my position as an "adolescence expert" and despite the knowledge and proficiency that comes with the experience of raising two teens, I still struggle with the disruptions that my family goes through as my teens grow and develop every day. I struggle because it's hard to stand firm on a constantly shifting platform. But we've learned as a family to adjust and to appreciate that the very fact that my teens are able to argue and question, and that they expect their voices to be heard, reflects development; and that forward movement makes my family better and stronger.

And Then There Is Sleep

Another major shift that occurs as our children reach adolescence concerns their sleep patterns. Sleep schedules and wake-up calls may not seem significant enough to deserve their own section in a book, but let me tell you that they are. When you consider the sheer horror involved in waking a teen—the subsequent delays in school, work, meetings, and, of course, the stress involved in starting the day already late for everything, while simultaneously bickering with your teen—you'll see that changing sleep patterns are important all right, and you should know about them!

Do you remember the last time you "slept in"? What does that even mean, anyway...sleeping in? My younger brother points out that the inability to sleep past nine in the morning as an adult is a surefire sign that people are getting old. You're *really* old if you can't sleep past seven! By those standards, I'm in my nineties. I normally scoff at this type of youth-centered drivel, but you know what? My little brother just may be onto something.

Think back to when you were a teenager and could sleep the whole day. I remember being able to sleep until one or two in the afternoon and waking up completely refreshed—and later that same afternoon, taking a nap on the couch. My bed really *did* feel so much more comfy in the mornings when I was a teenager. Of course, this only happened if my parents weren't home—for some reason I still can't figure out, my mom and dad truly believed that a teenage kid sleeping past eight in the morning was the most insultingly disrespectful thing to do to adults who can't sleep. They would dish out heaping doses of judgment about time and my misuse of it: "You know the whole day is gone and wasted;

you can't get that time back...." This was offered with a steaming side of guilt as they inevitably brought up all the impoverished yet dedicated teens out there working right alongside their parents at manual labor jobs that start at five in the morning—working for pennies, all while your lazy ass was lying there in bed sleeping the day away. Sigh...those were the days. Now, the only way I make it to 8 a.m. without any type of sleep interruption is by way of a medically induced coma (read, Tylenol PM or Benadryl). Even then, I'm lucky if I make it to eight o'clock. Just one of the many perks of getting older, I guess. Thanks for the insight, bro.

The teens in my house, by contrast, seem to sleep for days on end. And, unlike my parents, I really don't mind. I am aware that as they transition through adolescence and into adulthood (where, of course, their ability to sleep will dwindle), their sleep schedule has shifted, and even after getting nine, ten, or twelve hours of sleep on any given weekend, they are still operating on serious sleep deficits. You may have noticed as your child hit the teen years that your effort to set a curfew regarding anything happening late into the evening—getting home, getting off the cell phone, or ending computer use by a certain hour—was met with major disagreement and rebuttals such as, "Mom, the party doesn't even start until eleven!" or, "Ugh, I'm *so* not tired at midnight and can't sleep, so what am I supposed to do, just sit there and be bored?"

Teens are usually wide awake at one in the morning and are ready, of course, to socialize with their friends, who are also awake at that time. For various reasons, their sleep patterns have shifted. Where are we, the parents? Sawing logs in the other room, pretending to wait up for them so that we can follow through with our deadlines and rules. Because they don't get to sleep in during regular school days, and because they are likely still texting when they are supposed to be sleeping at 1 a.m., waking them up on school days is not a pleasant job. Another understatement, I know. If you have a teen in your house who has to get up for school, you know exactly what I'm talking about. When I have to go in to wake my nineteen-year-old son at the ungodly hour of 9 a.m., it's like walking into a bear's den right in the middle of his hibernation. And no matter how gently or gradually I try to wake him, he will, with 99.9 percent certainty, be cranky as hell. So, I have decided that this situation, like many others with my teens in this rapidly changing landscape, is not as big a deal as I make it out to be. Simply put, as my children have morphed into teens, I have decided that I need to "roll with it."

There are so many other things that you must do and worry about as a parent that you need to put this behavior in perspective. Here are some tips to help make that adjustment: (1) remember how you felt as a teen and accept/respect that your teen is right there, right now; (2) try not to take your teen's growls and grunts personally when you have to face the cranky bear; and (3) get him an alarm clock and let him know that if he is late to school, work, or whatever, then *he* will have to pay the natural consequences. Natural consequences include: too many tardies may turn into absences, and too many absences could mean summer school . . . yuck! Or, too many late arrivals at work means no more job, and no more job means no more money to spend on going out. Adolescence is a perfect time for our children to start being responsible for their own actions, or inactions, as the case may be. When you let consequences take their course, your teen learns to be responsible and you, my friend, no longer have to fear being eaten by the bear every morning.

Light at the End of the Tunnel

By now, your cortisol levels may be sky high and you might be feeling a little on edge about this whole *parenting teens* thing—and I don't blame you. I know exactly how you feel; three of my four children have either gone through or are smack dab in the middle of this insanely chaotic and sometimes turbulent period we call adolescence. But I am here to tell you this: have faith, for there is good news. And I know this not only because I have experienced it myself, but also because it has been studied and proven by researchers around the globe. Are you ready for this? The good news is: *things get better and more settled, and everything is going to be okay.* Really. The fact is that the vast majority of people with teenagers get through this crazy developmental period just fine, with no severe or long-term detrimental effects to the family or to the relationship. The relationship between parents and their child not only remains intact, but, more importantly, it gets even better! It is really up to us, as the ones with the fully functioning frontal lobes, to not miss this opportunity to appreciate the small, positive things in life, as our teens transition into fully functioning adults.

We are often busy and overwhelmed by the breakneck speed at which life moves (and it seems to move even faster when you have teens), but perhaps we can use those mature frontal lobes of ours to be purposeful and thoughtful; to slow down just a bit, and take in what is going on around us. As your child goes through some monumental developmental shifts, you can begin to appreciate a new level of maturity in your love for one another that only serves to strengthen your future relationship.

Case in point: my daughter Suzie is in her twenties. She has graduated from college, is working on her career, and is living on her own. She has developed into a strong, intelligent, beautiful, independent woman, and I couldn't be prouder. Yet during her teen years, much like her sister Sophia and countless other adolescents, Suzie probably likened me to Mark Twain's intellectually deficient father. Oh yes, I remember like it was yesterday, just how she used to roll her eyes and mumble under her breath while storming off in a huff. Now, however, at least once a week we go out for margaritas and chat. Yes, I said chat...as in, a meaningful conversation, face to face, like real, grown-up people. She asks for my opinion on things and I ask for hers. She confides in me, and I in her. We are much more than just mother and daughter now—we are good friends. And the relationship we have now, although we had to go through the ups and downs of adolescence, was well worth the time, energy, and effort. I wouldn't trade it for anything, and I'm about to do it all over again with Sophia. So, buckle your seatbelts, parents, because although the ride may be a little bumpy at times, the best is yet to come...I promise.

2

What Could They Possibly Be Thinking?

Adolescent Cognition

Think back to when you were thirteen. Can you picture it? Now, think about the way you used to think. This is not a riddle or some crazy psychological experiment. I want you to think about how your thinking is different now, compared with the way you used to think as a teenager. Not just the content, because clearly as adults, we focus on things that perhaps did not occupy our thoughts as teens. Rather, think about the process itself, and the quality and efficiency of your thoughts. To say that both the quality and quantity of our thinking changes vastly as we get older is a huge understatement. The same is true for the changes in cognition when you compare a child's thought processes to those of an adolescent. In this chapter I will cover several issues that we nerdy psychologists love to ponder, research, and debate. I want to share with you how changes in the way teens think play out in real life when it comes to their perspectives and their decision making.

After reading this, you may even begin to notice some changes in your own child.

Thinking about the process of thinking is called metacognition. Don't let that word scare you off. Stick with me. What we will really be talking about are the huge cognitive developmental milestones that your child reaches when she hits puberty. We'll also cover a question that judges, juvenile probation officers, and parents alike ask on a daily basis: "If this kid is so smart, why does he do such stupid things?" We call this adolescent risk taking. But first, a story.

I walked into the living room one day to find my daughter Sophia and her younger brother Gabriel watching television and having a snack. Sophia was thirteen at the time, and Gabriel was three. Not two minutes after I walked in, Sophia accidentally knocked over her entire glass of milk, spilling it all over the floor. My tired, I-just-got-home-from-work-and-am-exhausted mom response was: "Oh, good one, Soph." Imagine this being said in the most sarcastic and agitated tone imaginable. Gabriel's response upon hearing my response: "Yay, Sophie...good one!" He clapped his hands as he said this to her in the most sincere and congratulatory way. My three-year-old was genuinely cheering for his sister, as though I had really just given her a verbal pat on the back. He witnessed the same scenario and heard my words, but he did not pick up on my sarcasm. Conversely, Sophia knew without a doubt that I was obviously not *truly* praising her for spilling the milk, and responded with an appropriately defensive "Ugh, jeeze Mom, it was just an accident!" Why is that? How can a thirteen-year old pick up on sarcasm, but not a three-year-old? The answer is cognitive development.

Cognitive Leaps

We psychologists make a big deal about cognition and the brain. We become quite giddy when another geeky researcher discovers something new about the brain and how it impacts our behavior. Developmental psychologists, in particular, get excited when we discuss how our brains and our thinking (and of course, our behaviors) grow, change, and develop over time, as we get older and more mature. What my little milk-spilling anecdote exemplifies is not how darn cute my kids are, though I must say they are, even when spilling milk all over my floor. Rather, it offers a good example of the major cognitive advances that occur from the time we are children to the time we navigate our way through the wondrous period of adolescence. The main advantages that adolescents have over children in their thinking are, first, they can now think about possibilities. What I mean by this is that children's thinking is typically based on concrete and observable events, whereas adolescents can now think of hypothetical situations and what "might be." Teens can think about future possibilities, along with different potential outcomes associated with those possibilities. So, for example, they can think about what career choices they have in the future and really begin to extrapolate what life would be like as a teacher rather than as a lawyer.

Second, adolescents can fully understand abstract concepts. As teens we become much better at going from abstract ideas to very specific points, a cognitive ability that we weren't very good at as children. Our range of thoughts has become quite expansive, and as teens, we can now think in broad, existential terms one minute, followed by laser focus on specific details the next. Teens have the ability to comprehend the higher-order abstract logic inherent in puns, proverbs, metaphors, and analogies. Think about the Disney and Pixar movies created for young children. These films are typically loaded with puns, metaphors, and double entendres that go over young children's heads. Teens and adults, however, catch the subtle humor with no trouble.

Consider the following scenario: Sophia (age fourteen), Gabriel (age four), and I were watching Pixar's movie *Cars* for the hundredth time, and we came upon the scene where, after finishing a race, Lightning McQueen is approached by two small female sports car fans. The two little red Miatas introduce themselves to Lightning McQueen, saying, "Hi, I'm Mia. Hi, I'm Tia...and we're your biggest fans...CACHAO!" simultaneously *flashing* him with their headlights. Just after the scene ended, my daughter Sophia exclaimed, "Sheesh, I can't believe they show that kind of stuff in kids' movies!" and Gabriel had no idea what she was getting all huffy about. What Sophia was so accurately picking up on, of course, was that Mia and Tia were Lightning McQueen's groupies and the flashing headlights were representative of...well, I think you get the picture. The cognitively astute teen in the house was incensed, and her little brother was clueless.

Why are these types of hidden messages incorporated in children's movies anyway, especially if those hidden messages are unreachable by the main audience? The answer is that moviemakers (and their creative team of cognitive psychologists) are well aware of the fact that, although the target audience is made up of younger, less cognitively developed children, dedicated and caring parents and even older siblings of said children will be forced to watch these movies over and over and over again. So, why not provide a little entertainment that the older, more cognitively mature audience can enjoy as well? Genius. One of the many reasons they make the big bucks!

Another way in which teens' thinking is superior to children's is that they can think in multiple dimensions, which means that they can now view situations in much more complicated ways, rather than one aspect at a time. They have gained the ability to see things as relative rather than as absolute. And they've begun to see issues from others' perspectives as well as their own. Young children see things in absolute terms, in either black or white, while teens can see all the gray in between. Because of this new-found intellectual skill, skepticism becomes common during adolescence, and teens begin to question *everything*.

They question, for example, why parents enforce some rules and not others, or why, when older brother got away with something, you treated him differently. They question whether facts are actually facts, as well as which information is consistently true and which is not. And, of course, they question the sources of information. Enter, parents. During this exciting time of cognitive advancement, your teen is doing an excellent job of monitoring the validity and reliability of your thinking, your decisions, and your behaviors—and he not only makes these judgments in the present, he thinks back to the past and makes comparisons across time. (Impressive. I told you this takes skill.) What this means, of course, is that we parents are now pretty much always on the defensive. Welcome to the joys of parenting a cognitively mature kid! This is where many parents begin to question whether this teen questioning is really a good thing or not. In chapter 3, we will go into more detail on how this phenomenon negatively impacts parents' nerves (as in a teen jumping up and down on her mother's last one) and how it triggers conflict between parents and teens.

Finally, one of the main advantages that teens have over children when it comes to thinking is that teens are now highly metacognitive. Adolescents are constantly monitoring their own cognitive activity during the process of thinking, which can lead to several things: increased introspection, where they think (a lot) about their own feelings and emotions; increased self-consciousness, where they obsess about what others think of them; and increased intellectualization, where they think about their own thoughts, intellectual abilities, and regularly flex their newly formed cognitive muscles. This is, as I mentioned before, a major achievement for teens.

I told you to remember that this is a *good thing*, right? Because all this intellectual success does not come without potential pitfalls. What also happens as teens grow in metacognition is that they can become extremely egocentric. You know what I mean. These are the times when parents think, "How can this person, whom I gave birth to and love with all my heart and soul, be so damn selfish? All she thinks about is herself!" How do I know parents think this? Well, because this thought has crossed my mind many, many times with my own daughter. Don't get me wrong, not all adolescents are equally egocentric, and most of them (including my own) can also be extremely caring and giving. But there are times when parents are simply astounded at the "me, me, me" kind of thinking that teens engage in. I know I am.

Another possible pitfall is something called the "imaginary audience." This is when your teen feels as though everyone around her, especially those who matter most (her peers), are watching and judging her every move. Teens can become so preoccupied with what others think of them that it can influence quite literally *every* move they make, either for fear of ridicule or simply to please and be admired by said audience. The imaginary audience influences what she wears, how she acts, and who she sees, and it also helps to explain the endless hours in front of the mirror.

When it comes to potential pitfalls, I saved the best for last: the *personal fable*. This one is a doozy. The personal fable is basically the notion that a person's behaviors, decisions, and experiences are unique to him, and when considering potential negative consequences of these behaviors, the person's response is, "Psssht, that won't happen to me." Imagine overhearing the following conversation between two high school boys just before a holiday weekend:

"Dude, did you hear about Matt getting totally busted for drinking and driving last weekend?"

"Yeah, man, what an idiot. I heard he got totally wasted on beer and freakin' Jäger shots at Olivia's party, then drove his dad's Benz right into a freakin' pole! He is *so* screwed, dude!"

"I know, right? So... what are your big plans this weekend?"

"Man, I borrowed my mom's car and I'm gonna trek it up north tomorrow to a big party that's supposed to be off the chain! I'm gonna get my drink on this weekend, baby!"

"Dude, aren't you scared you'll get busted like Matt did last week? I heard the cops are out to get us!"

"Psssht, man, that won't happen to me! He's an idiot and that's why he got caught. I'm smarter than that dude."

And that, my fellow parents, is an example of the personal fable. As you can see, this line of reasoning (if you can call it that) is flawed. But many, many teens out there use exactly the same logic (if you can call it that) in justifying their decisions and subsequent behaviors. To be fair, it should be noted that this erroneous reasoning is not limited to adolescents. Although teens seemingly corner the market on making bad decisions and taking ridiculous risks, some adults commit the same proverbial cognitive crime. More on that later.

Risk Taking

The personal fable is just one possible explanation for why adolescents may make "stupid" decisions and engage in sometimes dangerous and risky behaviors (I use quotation marks here because the word *stupid* is a relative judgment term—what may be stupid to some may be genius to others). When adults ask, in utter bewilderment, "If he is so 'cognitively advanced,' then why does he make such dumb decisions?" the answer is multifactorial. There are likely many combinations of variables that come together like a perfect storm and cause teens to put themselves at risk.

Before we go into other possible explanations for teens' behavior, let's consider the term *risk*. What do I mean by risky teen behavior? Skydiving, perhaps? What about bungee jumping? Despite the obvious degree of risk involved in those examples, what I am really referring to when I bring up adolescent risk taking are behaviors like driving while under the influence, racing other cars on dangerous roads, having unprotected sex with multiple partners, or using illegal drugs, to name just a few. Every semester I ask my adolescent psychology students to name some of the latest trends in risky behaviors amongst teens. In other words, what kind of risky things are teens doing *today* that seem popular among this group of people? And every semester, without fail, I am surprised by at least one new trend in risky behaviors. I know you are curious, so here are a few examples of some of the latest trends (you may want to sit down for this):

24

- Alcohol: "Vodka eyeballing"—when a person allows other people (friends at a party) to pour straight vodka directly into the eye, reportedly causing the person to feel inebriated much more quickly because the alcohol enters directly into the bloodstream through the veins in the eye. If this is not bad enough, another trend is to insert highly concentrated alcohol into other orifices (think, nether regions) for the same effect. Yes, it's true.

- Drugs: "Molly"—taking this drug, which is essentially ecstasy in powdered form (both are MDMA, stimulants), just before going to a party, a concert, or a club with friends, making the person feel as though *everybody* is her friend, *everything* feels good, and she is ready to party all night long.

- Driving: "Ghost riding" or "car surfing"—when a person exits his car while the vehicle is still in motion and either dances or runs beside or on top of the car, with no driver behind the wheel, causing a rush or thrill at having accomplished this feat, presumably in front of a bunch of other teens.

Making Sense of Teen Decisions

Now do you see why people use the term "stupid"? Are these examples alarming? Yes, they are. Are they real? Yes, they are. This does not mean, however, that every single adolescent engages in such behavior (I, like most parents, am 100 percent positive that *none* of my children would ever do anything this irresponsible and dangerous), but lots of them do. The question is, why? Before going into other possible explanations, consider this not-so-unlikely scenario:

John is a typical fifteen-year-old freshman in high school. His parents are out of town for the weekend, and he decides to have some friends over for a small gathering on Friday night. He tells a few friends, and they tell a few friends, and before you know it, there are more than fifty people at John's house that night. Some people brought beer, some brought booze and more people, and some brought other recreational drugs of choice. John realized that what was supposed to have been a small gathering with a few buddies was quickly getting out of hand—people were even upstairs in the bedrooms doing who knows what! He thought about asking people to leave or ending the party early, but decided against it. By midnight, one of the neighbors had called the cops and reported hearing loud music, seeing drunk kids in the yard, and smelling marijuana. The police busted up the party and made everyone go home. The house was totally trashed and John was dreading his parents' return.

Why did John continue the party even after he saw it spinning out of control? Why did he not simply turn people away? The answers tie back to risk taking and the resources that teens have at their disposal. In addition to the personal fable that John likely had playing out in his head, we must also think about his brain. Earlier I said that by the time a child is six years old, his brain is already 95 percent of its adult size. Researchers suggest, however, that one of the reasons adolescents engage in risk-taking behaviors is that the teen brain is not fully developed. The prefrontal cortex, which is the reasonable, thinking, and decision-making part of the brain—the part of the brain responsible for planning, organizing, judging consequences, and exercising self-control—does not fully develop until people reach their early- to mid-twenties. When you also consider that the parts of the brain that are responsible for thrill- and sensation-seeking behaviors mature around the time of puberty, it's easy to see why this "gap" in brain development has been implicated in teens' poor decision making and risk taking. Some researchers have likened this situation to "... turning on the engine of a powerful race car without a fully trained, skilled driver at the wheel."[1] Now, let's talk about the social aspects impacting John's decision. Clearly, peer pressure is at play in this scenario. His friends likely pressured John to keep the party going. But peer pressure is just the tip of the social iceberg. Imagine that it was you, a grown adult with a job and responsibilities, hosting the party with *your* friends, and not fifteen-year-old John. Would you, as an adult, have felt the same pressures and made the same decisions? Your answer is likely a resounding "no," and social science research would support your answer. Psychologists have shown that, although teens and adults go through the same decision-making process, whereby both select the option that minimizes cost and maximizes benefit, teens and adults differ in how they weigh social consequences.

Adolescents weigh the social consequences of a decision much more heavily than do adults. In John's case, the social consequences of throwing everyone out and shutting down the party would likely have been angry friends and acquaintances who possibly would have ridiculed him at school the following day. Because he kept the party going, he was likely met with, "Dude, that party was off the chain!" or "Did you hear about that party John threw, it was so crazy the cops even came. Awesome!" Adults, on the other hand, generally do not value the opinions of our peers quite as much as teens do. This is not to say that adults are socially apathetic; look at the number of grown men and women posting endless selfies on various social networking sites. I, myself, am a reasonably social person who likes to have a good time, but I can say with a fair amount of certainty that if I were throwing a party and my guests were trashing my house and breaking the law, I would not let it continue because I feared being called names the next day at work.

So, to sum up our teen's cognitive advancements, here is the bottom line: Our children are actually learning to think for themselves. Without even being totally aware of it, they are conquering several major cognitive milestones as they transition from childhood to adulthood. As teens, their thought processes and opinions may not completely match ours. In fact, we may, at times, be 100 percent certain that their thinking is faulty and perhaps even dangerous. But, guess what? It is *theirs*, so let them have it. What I mean is that of course, we, as parents, should guide them in the ways of logical reasoning and responsible decision making, but we should also give them the space and support they need to flex these newly formed cognitive muscles. It's like getting an awesome new game or toy for Christmas—of course they will want to test it out as soon as they get it! They immediately want take it out for a spin, just to see what it can do. Our kids may not start out being experts at the game, but given time and a bit of guidance and training, they will eventually reach a level of expertise that we can all live with and maybe even be proud of. So, how about we simply enjoy and appreciate who our children are now, and embrace the fantastic possibilities of the people they are becoming!

3

Storm and Stress

Understanding Parent–Adolescent Conflict

I *always* love my child, but sometimes I don't like her. That's right, I said it. And, if you were alone in a soundproof room, with no one around for miles, and were completely and totally honest with yourself, I think you would say that you sometimes feel this way too. Come on, admit it...it's okay. Around the time that your child begins the second decade of life, things start to change in a fairly dramatic way. He is entering the developmental period that has been dubbed the time of "storm and stress," and it's called this for good reason. Adolescence is a time of important transitions for both the child and the parents. One of the telltale signs your child is transitioning from childhood to adulthood is conflict. If you, as a parent, are already in the throes of dealing with adolescent angst, then you know exactly what I mean. If, on the other hand, you are still basking in the euphoric bliss of the childhood years, then I hope this chapter prepares you for the fun yet to come as your child transitions into the teen years.

The few times I've had open and honest conversations (as opposed to those where people talk about what great parenting techniques they employ and how absolutely perfect their teen is) about this topic, the parents involved end up feeling like fellow veterans who have been in the trenches together during an all-out war. Parents who have experienced the incessant and relentless bickering that is known as parent–adolescent conflict share a special bond, especially once they've gone through it and survived. Parents of young children may read this and say, "Come on, is it really *that* bad?" The answer is yes. Yes, it is. At least it *feels* that bad when you're going through it. I should note that, first, in the larger scheme of things, like when we compare it to world hunger, typhoons and earthquakes, or the suffering in impoverished nations around the globe, the conflict really *isn't* that bad. But many researchers have shown that when it comes to parent–adolescent conflict, parents are the ones who are left feeling the psychological and emotional fallout—much more so than teens. In fact, to teens, the constant bickering and squabbling may be a way to exercise their new cognitive abilities, strive for independent thought and opinion, and assert their new role in the family dynamic and make sure their voices are heard.

Second, there is a rare breed of family out there that, for various reasons, experiences very little, if any, conflict at all. Hard to believe, but it's true. But consider this: you visit the parenting section of your local bookstore; you look around and see the different areas divided into age categories. In the area devoted to infancy you might see titles like, *How to Bond with Your New Baby*; in the early childhood area, you may see titles like *How to Snuggle with Your Toddler* or *How to Nurture Your Growing Child*; and when you look over in the area for parenting teens, what do you see? You see titles like *How to SURVIVE Adolescence, Keeping Your Sanity with Teens*...or, better yet, you'll see mine. This is all for good reason: being the parent of a teenager is really hard. Parents of teens are desperately seeking answers to questions like: "Who is this big, moody kid and what did he do with my sweet little boy?" or "She used to love to snuggle, chat, and spend time with me, but now we are constantly bickering.... Why?" The point is that conflict between parents and their children is a reality that many (underscore the word "many") families experience as those children enter and go through the period of adolescence. I mean, they don't use words like "turbulent" and "raging" to describe infancy or childhood, do they?

Why War?

Psychologist and educator G. Stanley Hall first coined the phrase "storm and stress" to refer to the period of adolescence during which teenagers become moody, are in conflict with their parents, and engage in risky behavior. Thanks to many researchers in this field, there are several things we know about conflict between parents and their teens. As a researcher, I find this information interesting and informative, but as a parent, it makes me let out a huge sigh of relief. It's a great comfort to know that there are so many other parents out there experiencing the same issues, concerns, and battles that there is an entire body of literature to cover it.

We know that it's natural for teens to create both physical and emotional distance from their parents. This is what we are programmed to do as independent human beings, and our teens are no exception. This happens as they set out on their adventurous quest to establish themselves as individuals, to form their own identity, and to be independent and autonomous—all separate from their parents. They are seemingly hell-bent (with good reason) on establishing their own thoughts and formulating their own opinions, and they demand to be heard—and when I say demand, in some cases, it really is a demand. As many of us know, we parents may have a knee-jerk response that is not too welcoming to these teen demands. At least, that is my experience. Nevertheless, as parents of these brave explorers, we don't take kindly to all of this distancing business because what we see is our little girl (in a big girl's body) trying to do things on her own, and it makes us nervous, afraid, and protective. Plus, we cling to the memories of when she used to love sitting on our lap and reading stories.

So, how do you respond to this push for independence that seems to be creating a rift between you and your teen? You may voice your concern and try to protect your child from making mistakes by having (or at least trying to have) nice, long conversations with her; or you may try to keep your teen close by requiring family time, in the hope that he will see the big picture and, by spending time with the people who love him and gave him life, will snap out of it. In the end, the result of these attempts is usually parent–adolescent conflict. Essentially, parents try a variety of strategies to avoid or escape the constant bickering, because who wants all that noise? Nice try, parents.

Conflict typically increases as children enter early adolescence (at ten to thirteen years of age), tends to level off at mid-adolescence (fourteen to seventeen years), and usually decreases in late adolescence (eighteen to twenty-two years). There are several explanations for why conflict increases during the early teen years, starting with those darn raging hormones and extending to teens' demands for autonomy and independence or even straight-up death-defying rebellion. The truth is, there are various combinations of factors that contribute to igniting the fiery flame of parent–adolescent conflict in the early teen years, including puberty, personality, cognitive shifts, social context, peer influences, and many more. In early adolescence, teens can be somewhat moody and self-centered, while also keen to exercise their newly acquired cognitive tools by arguing every point and taking on every battle. Combine all of this with the fact that parents are tired, stressed, and dealing with their own issues too, and you can guess that the result will likely involve a quarrel at minimum, and full-blown war at worst.

My daughter Sophia and I are at odds quite a lot, and one reason is that she and I are both strong-willed, intelligent, outspoken women, who have no problem asserting themselves. All good things, right? Ah, but here is the problem: we are *also* both stubborn, opinionated, and ready to go to the mat for what we consider a justified reason. That reason, of course, is that we both think that we're right and the other is wrong. Of course, dear reader, we all know who is *really* right, don't we?

The good news is that as parents we learn to manage conflict with our teens as they reach middle adolescence and we begin to feel a bit more like we're in a semi-amicable relationship with another human being once they reach older adolescence. This is just about the same time that our teens begin to realize that our IQ has risen and their parents aren't as idiotic as they used to be! In the Adolescent Psychology class I teach, I always ask

33

my students why they think conflict between parents and their teenage children decreases after the teens reach age eighteen. Any guesses? The first response is inevitably: "They move out of the house," which is, in part, true. As teens hit older adolescence, they broaden their social and circumstantial horizons by either going off to college, moving out, or getting a job, which provides more space, physical and otherwise, for all to gain a little perspective. In this case, at least, the heart grows fonder with a little absence—or at least a little less in-your-face bickering.

What also happens in late adolescence is that your child gains perspective and also becomes significantly more mature—not just physically, but cognitively, socially, and emotionally as well. It's as though her brain and heart finally catch up to her body. Now these well-rounded, mature children of ours begin to appreciate us as individuals. They not only have this newfound appreciation for the way you manage to do a great job at work, kick butt at being a good parent, and perform all things with superhuman strength, they also begin to look back and realize that they just might have been a royal pain in your rear end during their early teen years. So many of my students, after learning about parent–adolescent conflict and parents' perspectives, say that they are going straight to the florist and sending their mother flowers! So, in the event that you randomly receive a beautiful bouquet accompanied by a sweet note of appreciation from your older child . . . you are welcome.

Another thing we know about conflict between parents and adolescents is that, in terms of *what* parents and teens argue about, disputes typically aren't over significant, life-changing issues like educational or occupational goals, moral values, or ethical standards. Conflict between parents and teens is usually over everyday issues such as homework, chores, getting along with siblings, and choice of friends, music, or clothing. These are the times that you hear yourself saying things like, "Didn't I ask you to pick up those dirty socks off the living room floor nine times already?!" Or, "You're wearing that itty-bitty, microscopic skirt to school?...I don't think so. Get back in there and change into something decent, young lady!" Most teens then come back with a multitude of rapid-fire responses, all, of course, dripping with a sarcastic, snarky, or condescending attitude, which only fuels the fire. (I think they love to fuel the fire and "get a rise out of mom"—I've heard teens admit this!)

What's really interesting is that researchers have noted that, in the context of parent–teen conflict, parents tend to focus on social expectations and norms, whereas teens tend to see the issue over which they are arguing as a personal statement. For example, the mother of a fifteen-year-old girl who just got a matching green Mohawk with her best friend may say, "Good Lord! What are the neighbors are going to think, that I've raised a completely insane, green-haired hooligan?!" Or, when grandma is due for a visit: "Your room is such a pigsty!...now, go and clean it before your grandmother comes over and thinks I've raised you in a barn!" Parents' focus tends to be on how others will judge them as parents and on how family behavior fits societal norms. Not all parents think this way, at least not consciously, but some certainly do. Conversely, teens' responses might go something like this: "This is *my* hair, *my* body, and *my* room...and I should be able to color my hair green or poke holes in various body parts if I want. Hello, I am making a statement here! Screw what the neighbors think!" In other words, teens couldn't care less about social norms or standards; in fact, they may love inciting neighborhood talk about how far out the green hair is—that's the whole point. Teens' focus is on their independence and their personal thoughts and opinions.

Interestingly, we also know that of all the possible dyads in the family: father–son, mother–daughter, father–daughter, mother–son, etc., the mother–daughter relationship is the most conflictual of the bunch. Fascinating, right? Why is this? There are many proposed explanations for this, including that mothers and daughters have an especially strong bond and they feel that nothing can break it. So when it comes to arguments, the gloves can really come off, because moms and daughters know that there is no risk to the long-term relationship. My daughter and I know that I will always love her and she will always love me (notice I didn't say *like*); we also know that we can't ever divorce each other, as I will forever be a fixture in her life. So when it comes to conflict, heavyweight champs Frazier and Ali got nothing on us when we step into the ring. Ding, ding!

Another explanation for the especially conflictual relationship is that mothers and daughters have many things in common, including but not limited to their gender, habits, social roles, clothes, personalities, hormones ... the list goes on. In some cases, mothers and daughters are so much alike, and are around one another so much, that interactions can get more than just a tad annoying. Again, my daughter Sophia and I are a textbook example of the conflictual mother–daughter dyad. Let me make one thing crystal clear, just in case she is reading this: I love my daughter with every single cell in my body. But I confess that I have to remind myself of that fact sometimes, because we bicker, and sometimes even fight, pretty much every day.

One day, after a particularly heated exchange with Sophia, I met some fellow mom friends for postwar margaritas and proceeded to vent about how exhausting I found the all-too-regular conflict with my teenage daughter. My venting session ended with a frustrated *"Why does everything have to be so *@#^ difficult with my teen daughter?,"* to which my friends smiled and responded, almost in unison: "Because she's just like you!" What traitors my friends are. I will admit that my daughter and I are indeed opinionated, outspoken, stubborn, and passionate. The world practically comes to a standstill when we argue over Sophia wearing my socks! Onlookers may *think* it's because we're so much alike, but I know the truth. And the truth is...I'm right, and I'm the mom.

Context and "Emergency" Situations

When it comes to tough situations between parents and teens, one of the things we should keep in mind is context. In other words, think about the setting in which all of the bickering and stress occurs. Too often, parents believe that the increase in conflict or negative events indicates, by definition, a decrease in love. Not true. Of course our teens still love us. In fact, it is because they love us that they look to us for guidance and take us to task...it is their job. My guess is that it was once your job, too. You may recall, when you were a teen, questioning your mom or dad. Regarding context, I've also mentioned the simultaneous stressors that parents may experience while dealing with teen angst—they may also be facing job stress, physical fatigue, and other pressures—which makes incessant bickering over seemingly meaningless things extra stressful. (We'll talk more about this topic in chapter 9, as we discuss the "sandwich generation.")

Yet another contextual circumstance to consider is perspective.

In this case, perspective refers to the way teens interpret and react to situations, compared with their parents' viewpoint. Often, it is the difference in perception and the way we react to a certain event or circumstance that triggers conflict between parents and teens. Case in point: What is "an emergency"? And, other than arguing with their kids, how can parents react to their teen's "emergencies"?

From our perspective as parents, we often wonder, "Why does it seem that *everything* with my teen is an emergency? Just within the past twenty-four hours, I've received several 911-like calls from my teens." Here are just a couple of examples:

1. Before leaving the house one morning, I asked my seventeen-year-old daughter three separate times if she was ready and if she had everything she needed. "All good," she said. So, after dropping her off at school (which is thirty minutes from our home), I was halfway to my yoga class (to de-stress and prepare myself for the next set of emergencies), when I got a call: "Mom, I forgot my uniform for the hospitality program! And, the bus leaves in forty minutes! And, if I don't get it by the time we leave, I can't go! And if I don't go, I'll have to sit at school in the library for three whole hours with nothing to do!"

Being the dedicated mother I am, I seriously *considered* scrapping my yogi guru aspirations so I could go pick up the uniform. *What went through my head within a few seconds*: even if I did rush all the way back home and drive all the way back to school to drop off the uniform that *she* is responsible for, I wouldn't make it in time. Plus, I'd have to forgo yoga (aka: relaxation, exercise, and sanity) to rush around like a crazy person, fight traffic, and take on even *more* stress and insanity? All while relieving my daughter of any responsibility? Let me consider that for a moment...that would be a definitive "no." *What I actually did*: I calmly explained to my teen that she should see the natural consequences of her actions (being "stuck" in the library) as an opportunity to catch up on homework and maybe even get ahead. What a concept! And, perhaps she would learn the larger lesson, which was that it might pay to be a just bit more responsible next time—I suggested, "Write yourself a note or put the uniform in the car the night before"...not well received.

2. On my way to work, I got a phone call from my teenager, who was yelling, "Mom! Dad's out of town and the dog sitter is at his house trying to get in, but she's locked out because stupid Thomas (her brother, my teenage son) used the latch and the key doesn't work! And he left the garage door opener in the house, so there's no way to get in! And, if we don't get in, the dog will DIE! I told Dad I would take care of him. Mom, you have to do something!"

What went through my head: first, how did we go from zero to a full-blown, four-alarm fire in a matter of seconds? Second, why am I involved in my ex-husband's dog sitter being locked out of his house and what exactly does my teenager think I can do about it? Third, why is she acting as though a massive, blazing asteroid is hurling itself directly at her father's house, about to obliterate the poor helpless mutt inside? *What I actually did*: I told her to calm down and take a deep breath. I ever-so-gently reminded her that this is not my responsibility, but that the dog would be fine, and she will simply have to call the dog sitter and tell her to unlock the back door. What? Why must this be so difficult? Whew. Another crisis averted!

When parents of teens receive those types of calls (whether on a daily basis or hardly ever), an instant physiological reaction takes place. Really. Our cortisol levels spike through the roof, and we immediately feel compelled to either put on the gloves, get in the ring, and don our parenting superhero cape to save our child or, alternatively, fly like the wind and get as far away from this situation as possible (this is the famous fight or flight response). I mean, I'd like to *think* that my daughter likens me to Wonder Woman, ready and able to fix any problem with my magic lasso and those cool bulletproof bracelets, but guess what? It is *our* perception and *our* response that makes the difference between the fight, the flight, or reinforcing that independence and autonomy that teens are after. Sometimes, they don't actually *need* saving. And, sometimes, if they do, maybe they need to save themselves! Clearly, not every situation warrants a code blue, drop-everything-and-leave-right-now response, yet I do want my children to know that they can count on me, conflict or no conflict.

Just as with the notion of unconditional love, where we show our children that we love them no matter what, we need to let our teens know that they can count on us, even if it means we must run all over town like a crazy person sometimes. Our perceptions and subsequent reactions really make a big difference in the way these types of "emergencies" play out. Handling these situations in a positive, less discordant way is not easy, and can certainly be inconvenient and stressful for us parents, but the positive effects for our teens can be far-reaching and extremely beneficial. And we may even reap the added benefits of avoiding daily battles and imparting a life lesson or two along the way.

So, the next time you get one of those 911 calls from your teen, take a moment to think through the situation. Is this a teaching moment or do you really have to bust out the superhero cape? How do we know? Perhaps you can ask yourself the following questions when faced with the next teenage crisis:

- If I take my teen's emotions and reactions out of the equation, is this truly an urgent situation?
- What was the cause of this difficult circumstance? Is it something that could have been avoided if my teen had done something, or avoided doing something?
- What would happen if I did nothing? What are the natural consequences, and could my teen stand to learn something from them?
- What would happen if I do step in and take care of the situation? Am I teaching my teen to be responsible, or teaching him/her to assume that I will always tackle the tough situations for him/her, and is this essentially robbing him/her of a valuable life-lesson?

The bottom line is that this can often be a tough call. Clearly, we want to help our children when they truly need us, but we must also remember that it is also our job to teach them about good decision-making, responsibility, and potential consequences to one's own behavior. I know it's hard to see our children struggle and perhaps even fall a time or two, but just remember that when the sirens really do go off and you are seriously called to save the day, the cape is there and ready to go.

Happy Endings

Because all good stories have a happy ending, I wanted to end this conflict chapter on a positive note. There are several optimistic and encouraging points to make regarding parent–adolescent conflict. First, despite the frequency with which parents and teens have disagreements, the good news is that these conflicts are typically not super intense or volatile. Arguments between parents and teens are usually characterized by incessant bickering or squabbling, which is why, for *some* parents, it seems like slow torture. It's not relationship-ending or life-threatening fighting, it's just tedious and exhausting.

The second piece of good news is that the conflict that parents and teens experience is generally not indicative of major problems for either the individuals or the family. In fact, research shows that of all the families that have adolescent children, only a small minority of them experience long-term problems or serious concerns. I often present on the topic of parent–adolescent conflict to parent groups and organizations around the country, and when I get to this "good news" part of the talk, I can almost hear a collective sigh of relief from parents in the audience. Believe me when I say that I understand all too well that when our kids are in the midst of this turbulent time we call adolescence, we parents can be genuinely concerned about our future relationship with our son or daughter, given all the bickering. But I am here to tell you, both from experience and from research, that all will be well.

There *will* come a time when you and your grown son or daughter look back and laugh at all the silly quarrels you had over socks and laundry. You may even get to a point when you miss the bickering. No way... really? Really. My daughter Sophia, who, as you have gleaned, has been the star of this chapter, is moving away to college soon, and the thought of not being able to engage in daily banter, debate, or even arguments with her makes me tear up a little. Ironically enough, you and your child may have actually benefited from some of those arguments, growing as individuals and developing a deeper, more mature relationship. And, like the good veteran that you are, you will at that point be able to share your war stories with your parent friends in the hope that they can be fully armed and prepared for their own battles.

4

Independence Day

Teens Striking Out on Their Own

It is a run-of-the-mill Friday night. After a long and stressful week filled with work deadlines, meetings, multiple trips to the grocery store, and attendance at various kids' activities, I look forward to a nice, relaxing evening at home. I'm ready to put an end to the madness of the workweek and recharge the old batteries by being with the people I love most, in the familial space where I unfailingly find solace. I envision snuggling up on the couch with my children, a glass of wine in one hand and a slice of pizza in the other—mom and kids enjoying a fantastic movie marathon and laughing together as a family. Ahhh . . . so nice and so needed. But wait. This is too good to be true. What is wrong with this picture? Oh, I know. My Friday night fantasy did not factor in one important and inevitable detail: my teens have their *own* plans.

Before I even leave the office, my cell begins exploding with texts from my teens.

Teen #1: "Mom, I'm gonna hang with Alex tonight, cool?"

"There's a football game tonight, so we're probably gonna go."
"Oh, and I'll probably spend the night at her house...ok?"

Teen #2: "'Sup Mom. I'm at Shawn's. We're gonna chill for a bit." *Later, after I've made several attempts to get an update:* "Still hangin' with my friends, but after my girlfriend gets out of work, we're gonna do something, ok?" "Oh, and I'll probably stay at Jacob's, ok?"

So much for my comfy, cozy family lovefest. What was supposed to be a tranquil evening of family bonding turned into a very different scenario: me, with the dogs, trying to watch a movie but really just making sure, via text, that my children were still alive. Not exactly what I pictured.

What happens to our children as they get older? At one point in time, they loved spending time with us...didn't they? Okay, maybe not as much as I remember. Perhaps I am simply projecting my own domestic wants and emotional needs onto them (I am both a mom *and* a psychologist, after all), but I'm pretty sure I'm not the only parent who has experienced the feeling of "being dumped" by her own children. As they approach their teen years, our children begin to shift their social focus. You remember how it was. All of a sudden, you felt this desperate need to be away from your parents, to prove that you could stand on your own two feet; you were determined to make your *own* decisions, without anyone, especially your parents, telling you what you could and couldn't do. Guess what, mom and dad? Now it's our children's turn, and they are feeling *exactly* the same way we did back then! Funny, how time changes some things, but others—like teens being compelled to get away from their parents and build their own identities and "do their own thing"—not so much.

Two things happen during early adolescence with respect to

how (and with whom) teens spend their time: first, they begin to seek independence and autonomy like a starving person frantically searching for food; and second, they begin to spend less time at home with family and more time out with their friends. Chapter 6 is devoted to friendships, peer influence, and the social world of teenagers. For now, let's tackle the issue of independence.

There is absolutely nothing new about teens wanting to be independent. In fact, this is a very old story. Your parents experienced this when they were young; you went through it; and now your child has been bitten by the freedom bug. We all, ultimately, want to feel as though we have our own thoughts, our own opinions, and our own voice. It's human nature. We want to be our own person and make our own decisions, independently from our parents. Surely, you can relate (think hard about your parents' rules growing up—you will likely remember the feeling of rebellion!).

The real issue is perspective. Once we switch roles and we are no longer the developing young person but rather the old-fogy parents, we find ourselves a little lost. Wasn't it just yesterday that our wonderfully dependent young children not only wanted, but *needed* us to be there for them at all times, to help, to support, to teach? And we absolutely reveled in being needed, because it felt good. It fulfilled all kinds of basic biological and evolutionary needs that come with perpetuating your very own species. You remember the feeling, don't you? It was simultaneously horrifying and intoxicating to think about your child's absolute reliance on you. Until now, our definition of what it meant to be good parents was based on being ever present and simply being there for our children, as we found comfort in their complete dependence. So it is unsettling, to say the least, when our child, who used to need us and who wanted us to be there at all times, makes it painfully clear that now he does *not*.

At the risk of sounding like an academic snob, I would like to offer a semantic distinction. The word "independence" refers to a person's *capacity* or *ability* to behave on her own. Clearly, as our teens become physically and cognitively more mature—stronger and smarter—of course they are *capable* of doing things on their own. But, to capture the more nuanced description of behaviors, thoughts, and beliefs associated with teens' desire to strike out on their own, I prefer to use the word "autonomy." Because teens do this in a variety of ways and in a multitude of contexts, we will break this concept of autonomy into the three separate categories that psychologist and researcher Larry Steinberg refers to as emotional, behavioral, and values autonomy.[1]

Emotions

When teens strike out to establish their own feelings and opinions—about people, places, and things—they gain *emotional autonomy* from their parents. This is a big deal for them. Unlike the good old days, when they blindly liked a friend with whom you set up a playdate, they now want to judge and decide for themselves whether a person, be it a peer, coworker, or even (gasp) a new romantic interest, is worthy of their emotional investment. They ask themselves: Do I like this person, or not? Does this person make me happy? Do I love this person? Should I be angry at him for being such a jerk? Note that this decision-making process is not predicated on whether their parents like/hate the person—teens' focus is on the fact that it is *their* choice. That is the whole point! What makes this a bit menacing for us as parents is that we know our child can get hurt. We pride ourselves on our unwavering devotion to protecting our children. It's coded in our genetic makeup, for cryin' out loud. So when we see our child become emotionally invested in someone, whether we like or approve of the person or not, all while knowing there's not a darn thing we can do about it, we feel vulnerable and we worry incessantly. It is one of the things that binds us in our experiences of raising teens.

Ironically enough, one way of gauging whether teens have reached emotional autonomy is observing whether they have "de-idealized" their parents and begun see them as normal people. That's right...I am referring to us falling from that beautiful pedestal of omnipotence that our kids had us on when they were very young (feel free to reread chapter 1, but you may want to grab some tissues first!). In establishing their own emotional autonomy, adolescents evaluate the extent to which they depend on themselves rather than their parents when making judgments and trusting their own feelings. It's the teenage version of the Little Engine That Could: "I think I can, I think I can..." Teens newfound ability to make their own judgments not only serves to establish emotional independence but also helps to forge identity and boosts self-confidence and self-esteem—which are all good! The goal for our children as they transition to adulthood, whether we like it or not, is to successfully individuate from us. After all, once they go through puberty, our kids look older, they act older, and they want to be treated accordingly. All of this typically causes us as parents to cringe and collectively bury our heads in the sand in a grand effort to maintain blissful ignorance.

Sophia and I are often on what seems to be opposite sides of the emotional spectrum, but what I am called to do is accept the fact that, by wanting to formulate her own feelings and emotions, separate from mine, she is doing her job at navigating this developmental journey we are all taking part in. You notice I did not say that I have to enjoy, agree with, or even understand her feelings; rather, I should appreciate and support her experience. A bit touchy-feely, I know, but I speak the truth. Easier said than done? Most definitely. But the result will be a happy, healthy relationship between you and your teen . . . and what could be better than that?

Behaviors

In attaining *behavioral autonomy,* adolescents not only seek to make decisions on their own, they also strive to follow through on those decisions, *independently* from their parents. I know what you're thinking: *my* teenager? Make a decision *on his own?* And follow through with it? Indeed, that is what I said. I'm not talking about *you* making the decision *you* feel is best for your teen and expecting him to follow through—for example, me deciding that it would be good for my teenage son to volunteer at the local food bank and expecting him to make that happen. I'm talking about *your teen* wanting to make decisions for himself and having the wherewithal to see it through. This is huge, for both teens and parents. It is huge for teens because it can give them experience, build confidence, and make them responsible (even when they fail). It also gives them a sense of freedom and offers at least the impression that their parents support them and believe in them. All positive things, right?

But parents' perspectives and experiences may not be quite so positive. Allowing our teens to make decisions for themselves is huge for us as parents, because when we envision our newly minted teen faced with making a decision on his own, our brains are flooded with "what if" scenarios: *What if* he makes the wrong decision and gets hurt? *What if* she puts herself in danger because of her decisions? *What if* he does something so stupid that it jeopardizes his entire future? How do I know that these things might cross your mind? My own teenagers have made me the master of what-if scenarios, and I have spent many a sleepless night worrying about whether my children will "do the right thing," while praying to any and all celestial or magical beings that the kids come home in one piece.

The bottom line is that we parents know too much; and we know that our teens know too little. After all, we were teens once, too. And if we are brave enough to admit it, when we think back on some of the idiotic decisions *we* made back then, at least some of us would conclude that it's a miracle we're alive today. Come on, fess up...you are amongst friends! As people who have made embarrassingly stupid decisions ourselves and lived to think about them, we understand certain things with a clarity that comes only with years of experience. We know, for example, that our teens' brains are not fully developed and that they still lack the ability to think things through effectively and weigh benefits and potential consequences when making decisions. We also know that, because of peer pressure and other social influences, teens are more likely, when compared to (most) adults, to engage in risky behaviors that may cause harm or even worse. We know about predators, and we pray our teens will make decisions that will keep them safe. We know that accidents sometimes just happen, and, well, there is nothing we can do about that—and that realization drives us even more nuts! I could go on, but I think you get the picture. We have so many justifiable reasons to worry about letting our teens make their own decisions, it's a wonder we get any sleep at all, ever.

But here is some information on teen decision making that, thankfully, gives us hope. As our teens navigate their way through the tricky developmental period of adolescence, their decision-making abilities improve. By the time they get to older adolescence (around age seventeen), they become more aware of risk, they get better at considering future consequences, and they seek advice and input from trusted and reliable sources. Sure, they are more susceptible to peer pressure during their early teen years, but here is some more good news: around middle, and certainly by late, adolescence, they are less likely to conform to peer pressure, even as the pressure to "follow the crowd" increases at this age. And the best news yet is that we parents remain more influential than our kids' peers when it comes to important, long-term issues like core values and belief systems. Their friends' opinions matter more in the areas of day-to-day life, such as the type of music they listen to and the clothes they wear. Bottom line: parents still matter when teens make decisions about important stuff! Feeling a bit relieved? Good.

Values

Now, onto *values autonomy*. When our children are young, we try to instill in them the ability to recognize the difference between right and wrong, as well as the importance of considering others and being civic minded. And, to a certain extent, they get it. But it's not until adolescence that they gain a more mature and comprehensive understanding of moral reasoning and ethical dilemmas, along with a sense of the importance of religious beliefs and altruism (helping others). Researcher Lawrence Kohlberg suggests that humans develop the ability to make moral judgments in a stage-like process. He asserts that when we are faced with morally or ethically ambiguous situations, really young children make decisions based on the notion of consequences and rewards. In other words, they do good things with the motivation of getting positive verbal strokes or that elusive gold star, and they avoid doing bad things for fear of getting scolded or put on the naughty list.

As they mature, teens reach a point at which their decisions are based on moral reasoning that is much more abstract and complex. They not only take into account societal rules, laws, and expectations, they also begin to think about issues in ways that transcend social norms. Their prosocial reasoning becomes much more sophisticated and they are able to truly understand what is right and wrong on a significantly broader and more inclusive scale. They are now able to identify, for example, that an act of kindness or some other form of altruistic behavior is good, regardless of any other political or legal standard stating the contrary (think of giving money to a homeless person, despite it being illegal). This is all good, except for the fact that research also shows that, although teens gain a theoretical understanding of right and wrong and can think through social issues with the newfound certainty of a moral absolutist, their actual behaviors do not necessarily reflect their logic. Most teens predictably continue to focus on themselves and behave in very egocentric ways, engaging in ostensibly selfish acts. So, despite advances in some areas (i.e., moral development), we must remember that teens still have deficits in other areas (i.e., adolescent egocentrism) and consequently, it is often the case that teens' level of understanding does not match up with their actual behaviors.

The other area in which our teens blossom when it comes to

values autonomy is in the realm of religious and spiritual beliefs. I clearly remember being a wide-eyed, seventeen-year-old freshman in college, and finding out for the first time in my life that there were religions in the world other than my own. Up to that point I had indeed led a numbingly sheltered life, but hey, you don't know what you don't know. I grew up in a very traditional, very Catholic, Mexican family, where our religious beliefs permeated everything from large, all-encompassing issues to the minutiae of daily life. Growing up, my brothers and I were pretty much surrounded by kids from other like-minded Catholic Mexican families, and these kids all, without question, wholeheartedly believed and behaved in exactly the same way that we did.

For me, my family's religion and my cultural identity were one in the same. But when I got to university and began to meet people from all over the world, I felt as though I had been observing life through a teeny, tiny peephole. Until that moment, I had no idea what I had been missing. Now, I had a full, open view of the different perspectives life had to offer, and I was desperate to take them all in. I remember spending hours in the university bookstore exploring new ideas. During one visit, I came across L. Ron Hubbard's book on Scientology and was absolutely fascinated by how vastly different it was from my own indoctrination. I never wavered in my own beliefs, and most adolescents do stay pretty true to the core values taught to them by their parents, but I will say that I began to explore different religions, diverse political viewpoints, and varied sexual perspectives during that time. And this is the point. As adolescents gain the cognitive ability to question and understand larger concepts, and then attain the freedom to explore and decide for themselves what *they* choose to believe, they achieve true autonomy and independence, and take one step closer to becoming the person they want to be.

A brief note of caution: when parents try to stifle their teen's desire for independence and autonomy, their efforts are more often than not met with resistance and rebellion. When you were a teen, did your parents ever lay down the law so emphatically that it sounded to you like an invitation or even a challenge? When teens hear parents say things like, "You are absolutely *not* allowed to..." what follows in terms of their behavioral response is usually not pretty.

I remember growing up listening to my seven aunts gossip and talk about other people—they would especially focus on the hoodlum kid of whichever aunt was not in the room to defend herself and her child. They would toss around judgment and rancor with ease, especially as it related to the kind of parenting that led to the horribly shameful behavior being judged at the time. One day, one of my tias proudly announced that her fifteen-year-old daughter was not allowed to wear makeup. "Oh no," my aunt declared smugly, as though the statement itself was a direct reflection of her parent-of-the-year award, "she is a natural beauty and she is a good girl, so she knows she is not allowed to wear makeup and she will obey my rules." Hmmm.

My cousin and I were both freshmen at the same high school, and what my aunt did not realize is that every morning after she dropped us off at school, my cousin would go straight to the girls' bathroom and cake on layer after layer of the cheapest, most hideous makeup you've seen any one person wear. I still liken it to a cross between an Insane Clown Posse and Tammy Faye Bakker face. What's worse, my cousin made it clear, in an act of over-the-top rebellion, that not only could her mother not dictate what she wore on her face, but she was not about to obey *any* restrictions. So she would also change into the kind of outfit I had only seen worn by professionals on the street! Needless to say, my cousin took on quite a reputation.

Moral to the story: allow your kids some latitude—let them explore and find who they want to be. Don't make anything the "forbidden fruit" that they feel they *need* to have at any cost. If you, as the parent of a teen, decide to take the absolute and punitive approach, don't be surprised if and when your teen does whatever you are banning anyway; or prepare for the possibility that your child will simply hide his behavior or lie about it. Please note that I said "some latitude," and not "complete, unrestrained freedom." I am not suggesting that teens should have no rules, limits, or boundaries. I am suggesting, however, that we, as parents of these already defiant group of kids, should think and behave strategically instead of emotionally when it comes to putting these boundaries into place for our teens. If we frame those rules and boundaries as absolutes, what we essentially do is lay down the gauntlet, almost daring our teens to cross that particular line. Remember, teens do love a challenge, especially when it comes to challenging their parents, with their seemingly insane and ridiculous rules! Consider yourself warned in the ways of the teen. To wrap up, our teens' goal of achieving true autonomy cannot be met if parents deny or resist it. On the contrary. In order to help our teens successfully reach independence, we must foster close and supportive family relationships with them, so they know, without a doubt, that they are loved and supported as they embark upon this trial-and-error period of emotional and behavioral exploration. Despite this daunting and seemingly colossal task, we as parents must support our children when they seek independence from us. Of course, they should know that with freedom comes increased responsibility. But we *should* encourage them to strike out on their own, while also maintaining emotional closeness with them.

Remember that we parents still have tremendous influence on our children, especially when it comes to the important and lasting things in life. Research indicates that adolescents report that they trust and respect their parents significantly more than they do their peers, especially when it comes time to make important choices in life. They look to us for guidance and unconditional acceptance, while simultaneously seeking independence and boundaries. Sound confusing? That's because it is! Being the parent of a teen means that our world is filled with confusion and frustration. Often, you may have no idea what to do in a given situation involving your teen, and that's okay. Believe me, you are not alone. But let me say this: if you simply take a step back and remember what it was like to be in your child's shoes, and also remember that loving and supporting your teen, no matter what, goes a very long way, the relationship will be one filled with mutual respect and admiration. And you, my friend, will beam with the pride of a person who has accomplished one of life's greatest feats: raising a decent human being.

Go On, Let Go a Bit!

We love our children with all our hearts. For as many years as they have been alive, we have invested countless hours, dollars, and sleepless nights making sure that they are safe and well taken care of. And how do these children repay us, as they reach adolescence?

By wanting to spend every waking (and even non-waking) moment with their friends. I mean, sometimes teens act as though spending time with the family is a punishment of the worst sort! Maybe it's just *my* teens who act like that, but here is the point: I know you don't want to hear this, but it's time to start letting go.

If part of the goal in adolescence is to become independent and autonomous—and it is—then parents must come to grips with not if but how they will begin to grant their teens the freedom they so desperately want. This is not easy. Often, we parents wonder if we're doing anything right. As you well know, parents of teens are especially plagued by such questions as: Should I let her go to the party—or is she too young? Should I let him go on that trip—is he responsible enough? How can I make sure she'll be safe? Will he be okay in college? How many times can I call or check in without being a nag? The reality is that we must trust ourselves *and* our children. Trust the fact that you have done a great job raising this kid so far and will continue to communicate and arm her with the information she needs to make good decisions.

We should also trust our teens and let them *know* that we trust them! Doing this sends them the message that it is okay for them to stretch their wings a bit and it gives them a sense of support and confidence. And let us not forget that no one is perfect! We should all expect that there will be slipups by both parents and teens, but guess what? Failure leads to learning and ultimately to success, so go on, parents, let go a bit. Gradually, you and your teen will figure out what works best for you, and in the end you will both be happy you did!

5

Tackling the Tough Topics

Talking to Your Teen About Puberty and SEX

Once upon a time, there was a fairy godmother who came to teach all the children in the land about what happens to their bodies as they get older. Parents of teens loved this fairy godmother. The children learned all about puberty and reproduction, and everyone lived happily and healthily ever after. *The end.*

As parents of young people whose bodies are undergoing tremendous physiological changes, we often *wish* we had a fairy godmother to help us with the seemingly monumental task of educating our children about puberty, sexuality, and reproduction. These are, without a doubt, some of the most difficult and complicated topics that we parents have to tackle as our children inevitably grow to physical maturity. Not only is it challenging, it can also be scary, embarrassing, awkward, and uncomfortable for all parties involved.

To be clear, I'm not simply referring to having "the talk" with your child, although that is part of it. Having "the talk" implies that you sit down with your child *one* day and have *one* nebulous conversation about sex that lasts *one* minute, and then it's over, never to be brought up again. Whew, glad that's over! What I'm referring to is helping your child understand the entirety of the pubertal process and the exciting (and sometimes horrifying) implications—physical, cognitive, and social—that come along with the physical changes of puberty. Perhaps we should see it as a journey. It's a journey that involves your child becoming a fully mature man or woman; a journey on which you and your child both realize that biological reproduction is now possible; and one during which you must begin to come to grips with the fact that she not only looks older and wants to be treated as older, but that others (namely those of the opposite sex) are now noticing that she looks older...and hotter. This is when moms want to hug their babies and lock them up in their rooms until they're thirty, and dads reach for their shotguns!

Imparting Knowledge

As you know, the significant journeys that happen in our lives don't typically happen in one day. Similarly, communicating with your child about topics such as sexuality and reproduction, ejaculation and menstruation takes multiple conversations and significant time, effort, and patience on your part. Sometimes a topic is thrust upon you (no pun intended!) and you have no choice but to tackle it, ready or not. For example, one day my daughter Susan came home from elementary school, and when I asked how her day was, she responded, "Mom, what is a blow job?" What the?? Hopefully, she was too young to decipher the look of horror on my face. She proceeded to explain to me using her sweet little fourth grade vernacular that she had heard a bunch of boys in her class saying this word and snickering, and she simply wanted to know what it meant. So, I told her. Honestly. Using the fourth grade vernacular referenced above, of course.

These conversations take perseverance, because teens usually dread these heart-to-heart, heuristic opportunities as much or even more than parents do. Sadly, all too often parents are either unable or unwilling to take this eye-opening journey with their children. The result is usually minimal communication between parents and their teens regarding puberty, relationships, sexuality, and reproduction. Why does this happen? There are lots of reasons, and we'll get to those soon. It should first be noted, however, that there are some parents who discuss all these issues, and more, with their children with the oratory ease of a poet, the careful skill of a counselor, and the informed wisdom of a great teacher. These parents begin encouraging their children early on to openly discuss body parts (using scientific names, not silly made-up ones like wee-wee or hoohee), bodily functions, development, and other issues associated with pubertal maturation, all without a hint of embarrassment or shame. To these parents: I salute you. It takes great courage and determination to keep our children truly informed, particularly when puberty and sexuality are not at the top of their favorite things to discuss with their mothers and fathers. So, keep it up. You are not only an inspiration to other parents, but because you set the example for your children, they will, in turn, be great communicators and mentors to their children. Last, please read on, as I hope to provide you with a little insight and perhaps even more tools for your parent–adolescent communication toolbox.

Despite what we would like to think, the reality is that most adolescents today are either ignorant (I mean this in the truest sense of the word) or misinformed about pubertal maturation and reproduction. I know this all too well. Every year, I teach a Human Sexuality class at the university, and because this class is always in high demand and because registration for it is usually on a first-come, first-served basis, the students I typically get in that class are seniors, as they get first dibs at registration. On the first day of each semester, I ask the students to write down anything that they want to know about sexuality. *Anything.* Because they usually begin the semester feeling extremely apprehensive, shy, and awkward, I assure them that their questions will remain completely anonymous and I encourage them to be open and honest in their requests. From that point on, we begin each class period by reading one of the randomly chosen questions and discussing the answer, particularly as it relates to what we will be covering in class. In addition to this practice being interesting and somewhat entertaining, it is a great academic exercise, as it allows me to provide information on issues that students clearly want to discuss, for which they are clearly seeking answers.

What inevitably shocks me is the nature of some of the questions. It becomes painfully clear to me that many of these older adolescents, despite being college seniors and somewhat "experienced," still lack very basic information not only regarding the act of sex itself (and all that involves), but also about their own bodies, reproduction, gender differences, and the emotions involved in relationships. To give you an idea of the types of questions students submit, I'll give some examples:

Female question: "When I use a tampon, does it go into the same hole as the one where my pee comes out?" **Answer:** No.

Male question: "Why do I feel horny ALL THE TIME? Is this normal? Do girls feel the same way, or am I just a freak?" **Short answer:** Testosterone, and yes, it is normal. Girls get horny too.

Female question: "Can I get pregnant if I have sex while I'm on my period?" **Answer:** Yes.

Male question: "If I'm getting hot and heavy with a girl, but I don't have any condoms, can Saran Wrap work in a pinch?" **Answer:** No.

Female question: "I'm trying to remain a virgin, but I want to show my boyfriend that I love him. I heard that if I only have oral and anal, that I'm still 'protected.' Is this right?" **Answer:** No.

Male question: "When me and my girlfriend have sex, I always pull out before I finish, this keeps us from getting pregnant and from STDs right?" **Answer:** No.

Male question and female question: "What is love and how do I find the real thing?" **No Answer.**

Now, keep in mind, dear reader, that although these questions may seem funny, scary, or even unbelievable, they are real, and more to the point, reflective of the dearth of information that even college seniors have. Also keep in mind that this could be *your* kid some day, sooner rather than later, so I respectfully provide these examples not to entertain, ridicule, or frighten you, but to illustrate the need for communication between children and their very first teachers—you.

Teens today tend to get most of their information about pubertal maturation and sexuality (the little information they have) from either friends or the Internet, and no matter how smart these friends are, and despite the vast treasure trove of data on the web, these sources are not always accurate or reliable. So, the real question becomes: What prevents us, as parents, from arming our own children with real knowledge about these sensitive yet tremendously important topics? After all, knowledge is power...we all know this. So, why is it so difficult?

No Judgment Zone

The first and most obvious reason we have trouble discussing sex with our kids is that sex (and anything remotely associated with sex) is an exceedingly taboo subject in our society. Because pubertal development, sexuality, and reproduction are all inextricably linked, they all become topics (under the larger umbrella of sexual behaviors) perceived by some as forbidden or even distasteful, specifically as they pertain to our children. In fact, there are entire organizations, be they religious, political, or social, that discourage a focus on topics related to sex (in any context, but especially in school) for fear of promoting or encouraging our children to go out and run wild. To this, I say hogwash! Granted, parents don't like thinking of their sweet little boy or girl as a sex god or goddess doing the types of naughty things we used to do when we were young, but we must learn to get a grip. Perhaps reflecting on the things we used to do is part of the problem. Our focus should be on arming our children with knowledge and giving them the correct information instead of relying on them to get it somewhere else.

Regardless of societal pressures and judgments, we parents will do more harm than good for our children if, instead of bravely and truthfully talking to them about sex, we choose to bury our heads in the sand and pretend that they are not interested in the topic. By resisting societal judgments and by embracing the undeniable fact that our children will inevitably develop into biologically, physically, and reproductively mature sexual beings, parents have the opportunity to raise well-informed, secure, and healthy adults. Social science research has shown that children become aware of sexuality much earlier than many people realize, as they are naturally curious about their own bodies and those of others.

My son Gabriel and his cousin Olivia are the same age. Ever since they were babies, they would take bubble baths together. They would giggle and play, truly enjoying each other's company, never noticing any differences between their naked little bodies. But one day, when they were around four years old, Olivia had an epiphany of sorts. After much observation, she blurted out, "Hey! I don't have one of those!" (pointing to Gabriel's penis), to which Gabriel replied, "Mom, why do I have one and Liv doesn't?" So, I answered. They hadn't realized the difference in their bodies, but once they did, they were curious and sought answers. They had finally made this grand discovery, and had a eureka moment.

We know that by the age of three or four children begin to explore their own bodies and perhaps even begin to masturbate.

Yes, I said the dreaded "M" word, and at the risk of having you slam the book shut, I ask you to consider this: When I mention children masturbating, am I implying that sweet little children are engaging in adultlike behaviors such as staring at a *Playboy* centerfold or viewing porn? Of course not. Young children begin to realize that certain things simply feel good. It is a very basic, physiological response. For example, have you ever been at a splash pad (park) and seen a bunch of kids huddled around one of the water jets, vying for position, trying to get the stream of water to hit a certain spot? This happens accidentally at first, then they realize that, hey, that felt pretty good. Or perhaps you've seen a kid (maybe even your own kid) spending a little too much time pressed up against the jets at the pool or in the tub? What I am describing is simply a matter of nerve endings and physiological bodily responses, so please do not confuse young children's behavioral responses with those of older adolescents' or adults'. Certain things just feel good, and we all know this.

The problem begins when parents, teachers, or society react negatively to the curiosity, causing shame and guilt. Consequently, children learn to disguise their interest and curiosity. Further research shows that the message "If it feels good, it must be bad," as it relates to sexuality, is often internalized by children at an early age, and can potentially lead to psychological and sexual disorders in adulthood. Thus, openly communicating with our children on a regular basis about their developing bodies, the pubertal process, and, yes, about S-E-X, without judgment or fear, behooves us all in ways that not only protect our kids from harm (teen pregnancy, sexually transmitted infections, etc.), but also puts them on a positive life trajectory. Our open and trusting attitude when handling these topics can have a lasting impact on the decisions our kids make and helps them build a healthy outlook around topics that are as natural as life itself.

Real Knowledge

Another reason parents shy away from talking to their teens about issues involving sexuality is that parents feel inadequately informed themselves. Human reproduction, sexuality, and puberty have all been occurring since...well, since the beginning of man (and woman!). But just because we've been doing it forever does not mean that we actually know what we're doing or how to explain it to our teenagers. As the Confucius saying goes, "Real knowledge is to know the extent of one's ignorance," but because sex is such a politically and morally loaded issue for some people, it is sometimes difficult for parents to muster the courage to become informed. In fact, a lot of parents rely on someone else to do the job for them...namely teachers. But guess what, parents? You assume that teachers will teach your teens what they need to know, in sex education or health class; but because of ethical or even legal reasons, teachers may not want to touch the subject with a ten-foot pole, so they assume that parents will teach kids what they need to know.

All the while, *no one* teaches kids critical information about sex, and they are left in the dark about salient issues that will inevitably play a big part in their lives. This is a real problem. Here is the good news: today we live in a world where we have an abundance of information literally at our fingertips. There are tons of accurate and reliable books, websites, and other resources to help us find out the information we need to help us communicate with our teens. I'd like to help get you started on your quest to become informed and motivated to talk to your teen about these tough topics by providing some facts that all parents should know. We'll call these the nitty-gritty, the 411, the scoopage of pubertal development and sexuality that you can now carry around with you in your communication toolbox.

- The average age for adolescents to start puberty in the United States still hovers around twelve years. However, puberty is occurring earlier for both girls and boys for various reasons.
- Girls start the pubertal process about two years earlier than boys do.
- One of the first signs of puberty is the adolescent growth spurt, where teens reach peak height velocity, followed by the development of the primary sex characteristics (gonads—testes and ovaries) and secondary sex characteristics (breasts and facial and body hair).
- Pubertal onset can begin as early as seven in girls and nine and a half in boys and as late as thirteen in girls and thirteen and a half in boys, and the time between the first sign of puberty and complete physical maturation can be as short as one and a half years or as long as six years.
- There are some differences in pubertal onset between ethnic groups: in the U.S., black teens begin puberty earliest, followed by Latino teens, followed by white teens, probably due to ethnic differences in income and/or weight, but possibly also due to exposure to chemicals that stimulate earlier puberty. Early maturation can bring social advantages (attention from prospective partners, popularity, proficiency in certain sports), but "early maturers" are also at risk for various issues such as more drug and alcohol use, delinquency, and early sexual activity.

- Some factors implicated in early pubertal maturation (especially in girls) include:

    o growing up in less cohesive families with more conflict;
    o growing up in households with no natural father, instead having a stepfather or other male not biologically related present (pheromones);
    o stress (small amounts of stress can speed up the pubertal process and a great deal of stress can slow it down).

- Once puberty has occurred, sexual intercourse can lead to pregnancy. Physically mature male and female adolescents are more likely to be involved in romantic activities with the opposite sex than less mature peers.
- Body fat composition can affect pubertal onset: obesity has been linked to early pubertal maturation, whereas extremely low body weight and/or excessive exercise can slow or even halt the pubertal process (for example, in ballet dancers, gymnasts, people with anorexia nervosa).
- Nocturnal emissions (aka wet dreams) are a type of spontaneous orgasm involving either ejaculation during sleep for a male or lubrication of the vagina for a female. They are most common during the early pubertal stages, but can continue past adolescence.
- Masturbation is completely normal and can actually be a healthy way by which young people can get to know their own bodies. Unlike what many think, men and boys do not corner the market on masturbation. Both males and females of all ages masturbate—we just don't talk about it!
- Most boys have experienced orgasm via masturbation before they have sex with another person. The data is less

clear for girls. There is a typical developmental progression of sexual behaviors that both boys and girls follow. The behavioral sequence for most American teens is: holding hands, kissing, making out, feeling breasts through clothes, feeling breasts under clothes, feeling a penis through clothes, feeling a penis under clothes or while naked, feeling a vagina through clothes, feeling a vagina under clothes or while naked, and intercourse or oral sex.

- There are many forms of birth control available, but the only way to protect against both pregnancy and any sexually transmitted infection is by using a protective barrier (condoms) or to remain completely abstinent.

Here is the bottom line, parents. Our babies are inevitably going to go through puberty, and they *will* become interested in sex. This is an undeniably beautiful and scary fact that we must accept. And we all know that if teens really want to find something out, they will turn to friends or the web to get answers, and often the "knowledge" they acquire from these sources is not exactly accurate or reliable. Why would they not turn to their parents, the people who presumably know a thing or two about the topics, given their lifelong experiences? After all, their parents have invested heart, soul, and finances into them their whole lives. Teens turn to other sources for information because, despite their parents' status as well-informed, intelligent, and experienced adults, the thought of having these types of conversations with their mother evokes in teens both emotional distress and physical disgust. My own daughter's response to me bringing up these topics: "Ewww, mom!" My son's response: "Mom, please don't...not again." Mind you, I've been getting these responses from my children even though I've been discussing these topics with them since they were young. But we should not let our kids' teen angst about tough talks with mom or dad deter us, for we are fierce warriors who do not back down from a challenge. And this, my friends, is the key: talk to your children. Talk to them early and talk to them often. It may be insanely awkward for all parties involved, but you'll be glad you did!

6

The Secret Society

Understanding Your Teen's Social World

Human beings are born to be social creatures. We persistently seek social interaction with and reciprocity from other human beings. We crave acceptance and love. We *need* friendships. As infants, we make sense of the world through social cues like the loving expression on our father's face or the soothing tone of our mother's voice. As we get older, we broaden our social sphere to include people outside of our small family circle. Thanks to our parents, we do this by attending preschool and/or joining playgroups, sports teams, and the like. By the time we reach our teen years, we have become fairly astute at friendship selection, and, in fact, given our newfound propensity for independence and autonomy, have made it priority number one. In this chapter, I attempt to shed a sliver of light on the secret society that is the teen social world. I will share with you some informative findings on peer groups and friendships, and the purpose they serve in our teens' developmental trajectory. I will also discuss the role we, as parents, play in our teens' social selections; and, of course, we will dive into the world of social networking and consider what the concept of friendship even means in that strange new realm.

Parents in the Dark

If you are anything like me, you often wonder just what your teen is up to during his free time. Who is he with? What are they doing? Unlike when he was younger and you knew exactly where he was and with whom, you now feel like an outsider looking into your own child's social world. It's a strange feeling, isn't it? The question we all wonder becomes: What exactly *is* this secret society, and, more importantly, *why* is it so secret? Let me begin by stating the obvious: When considering our teens' friendships and social activities, the parent and teen perspective is very different. We all know that as they enter into adolescence, one of the many significant shifts that occurs in our children's lives is that they spend less time with family and more with their friends. And, of course, one of our most basic fears is that we've been replaced... we're no longer needed. Sounds a bit melodramatic? Perhaps, but I know I've felt this way, and I'm fairly certain I'm not alone.

Parents' perceptions on this social schism are based on the way things *used* to be. What I mean by this is that because we, as parents of teenagers, now have a fair amount of expertise in anthropology, history, sociology, and all-around general knowledge, we tend to use our own social references and make comparisons when contemplating our teens' social world. First, we make the "When I was young..." comparison in order to make sense of current circumstances. For example, with respect to our teens' whereabouts, we tend to think: "When I was young, my parents never allowed me to hang out at a boy's house" or "When I was young, my parents used to insist on meeting my friends, and made family time mandatory!" Second, we make the "When my teen was little…" comparison. It goes something like this: "When he was little, he used to love spending time with us" or "When she was little, she actually appreciated the friends/clothes/activities I chose for her."

Finally, a third type of comparison we make involves social judgment. I'll call this the "What will they think?" comparison. In her work with parents and teens, researcher Judy Smetana points out that when faced with a conflictual social situation, parents typically focus on what Smetana calls social convention—that is, norms and standards as defined by friends, relatives, and other people—whereas teens typically see the same situation as a personal issue. For example, if your teen were to come home one day with a brand new lip piercing and state that she and all her friends decided to get one, Smetana hypothesizes that your typical reaction as a parent would go something like, "Good Lord! What will your grandparents think? What will the neighbors think?…that I've raised some sort of pierced-lip hooligan?" Your teen's response is likely to be: "This is *my* lip, *my* body, *my* decision…so I don't care what the stupid neighbors think!"

Clearly, what parents are doing when we make any of these comparisons is searching for some reference point from which to make a decision about our teens' changing social world that would fit neatly into our already existing experiences. We're searching for something that will help us make sense of the new and unfamiliar social landscape that we find ourselves in when our children reach adolescence; and because it seems the ground below us has become terribly unstable, we may have feelings of insecurity and doubt: "Am I doing the right thing? How do other parents handle this?" More on those types of feelings to come in chapter 9.

The Teen Perspective

As we discussed earlier, teens' perspectives on the social shifts are vastly different. Our teens are, all of a sudden, faced with a whole new world of social possibilities. This new world, which is experienced primarily in the school context, now affords teens opportunities to be liked, to be accepted, and, most notably, to be popular. Don't you remember how critically important these things seemed when you were in middle or high school? Friendships were certainly important when our children were younger, but this new social sphere in which our teens make their own selections quickly takes priority over time spent on just about anything else. As our children get older, their focus on friends and peer groups becomes entwined with their quest for identity formation and the way they want to be perceived by others.

Back when we parents were in charge of our young kids' social calendar, we would set up playdates and our children would experience friendships based on convenience (convenience, as dictated by *our* schedule and *our* adult choices). But as they become more independent and aware of various social choices, our teens want to make their own selections and break free from what they start to perceive as a social chokehold that parents have on their time. They no longer want to like someone because you're telling them to; rather, they want to decide for themselves who to like, who to call a friend, and what to do with their free time. As child psychologist David Elkind puts it, "friendships in childhood are usually a matter of chance, whereas in adolescence, they are most often a matter of choice."[1] Like it or not, this is what happens, so it behooves us all to remind ourselves of what it was like to be in our teens' shoes and maybe even begin to let go...just a little.

The transition from primary to middle school has serious social implications for our budding teens. Because adolescence is marked by the emergence of larger assemblies of peers, the pressure to be noticed, liked, and accepted by their cohort has never been more intense. The very nature of peer groups is in flux during adolescence, and several changes begin to occur in your teen's world. I've already mentioned the sharp increase in the time they spend with peers rather than adults. Another change that occurs is that peer groups begin to function much more often without adult supervision, and increasingly contact with peers is with opposite-sex friends. This is when, I imagine, many of you will start to squirm a bit; but do not fret, for this is not new, nor is it dire.

Not unlike when we were in school eons ago, if you were to walk into any typical middle or high school today, the social dynamics are such that you would see two types of peer groups, which researchers call *cliques* and *crowds*. Cliques are normally small groups of friends, and are defined by common activities or simply by friendship. These are the small groups of teens who have either known one another for a long period of time, perhaps because they live in the same neighborhood, or who all belong to the theatre group, cheer squad, or sports team. Crowds, on the other hand, are larger, more vaguely defined groups that are identified based on reputation, such as *the jocks, the nerds, the skaters,* and so on. Crowds serve an important purpose for our teens, as they are essentially a reference group for them. They contribute to the definition of norms and standards for such things as clothing, leisure activities, and tastes in music, and also provide a basis for a teen's own identity formation. In fact, despite being larger and less intimate than cliques, crowds have the capacity to impact teens' behaviors because teens want to imitate friends and be clearly recognized by others as belonging to this particular group.

Interestingly, all of this social growth and development is occurring during a time when our children are desperately trying to define themselves. Motivated by the ever-present imaginary (and maybe *not*-so-imaginary) audience and perpetual judgment of their peers, our teens are in hot pursuit of the identity they want to convey to the world. Almost as if by trial and error, they experiment with clothes, music, hairstyles, cliques, crowds, and even behaviors and activities. I clearly recall my daughter Sophia, upon entering high school, trying on different personas as often as she tried on different outfits for school. One week she was a *skater* chick, with all the accoutrements that accompany this style—big, bulky skater shoes (which, of course, cost me way too much money), low, baggy pants (the kind that drive all parents nuts), and, of course, the grungy, stick-it-to-the-man look that Tony Hawk has made famous. The following week she was trying her hand at being part of the *stoner* crowd, donning Bob Marley T-shirts and saying "dude" all the time, followed closely by the *geek* phase, where she insisted on obtaining, and very stylishly sporting, the nerdiest of black-rimmed glasses and, to my complete academic delight, was seen by her peers as totally cool for studying and making good grades.

Why do teens do this? What is the purpose of "trying on" these different guises and personalities, and just *who* are they trying to please? My guess is that you may already know the answer to this question. In large part, this is the way our teens learn to understand and accept themselves. It's true, but who are we kidding?

One of the major motivating factors in teens finding themselves and figuring out what they will wear, what music they will listen to, what behaviors they will engage in, and who they will choose to spend time with, is being liked and accepted by the people they want to associate with...their peers.

Some of you may cringe at the thought of your son or daughter's very personality being dependent on his or her friends. But, guess what? Peers, although they carry a fair amount of weight when it comes to the everyday, transitory stuff like clothes, music, and so on, have only *some* influence on the person your child will ultimately be. Parents play a key role in kids' friendship choices by socializing certain traits and predisposing their teens toward certain crowds—they do this in part by reinforcing specific interests and instilling particular values from the time their children were young. Parents also remain a significantly stronger reference point for more important things such as core belief systems (read, religious or spiritual beliefs, sociopolitical viewpoints, etc.). So, although your teen's friends will likely influence what she wears or what music he listens to, the good news is that you still matter most when it comes to who your child is at his core, and will indeed impact the larger, more significant decisions he makes in the future.

Having said this, it should be noted that the social arena in general, and your teen's peer groups specifically, serves a very important purpose. In fact, your teen's social interactions with peers help to promote normal psychosocial development, including helping with identity development and boosting self-esteem and confidence. As both a psychologist and a mother of teens, let me just say that this is a good thing. Peers tend to promote normal development in several ways. First, regarding identity formation, they serve as models and also provide feedback for members of the group. So, when Sophia was appraising the various peer groups (ie, skaters, stoners, nerds), she was essentially experimenting with her own identity and self-image. She modeled her behavior after individual members of the group whom she wanted to relate to, and she received feedback from them, which ultimately led to a decision whether to leave or stay with the group, therefore contributing to her own definition of self. I realize that to some this may sound like a bunch of psychobabble, but I assure you that this idea is based on years of research on teens just like yours and mine.

Peers and peer groups also assist in the development of autonomy. By their very existence, your teen's friends provide a venue for her to be her own person (complete with her own thoughts, feelings, and decisions), with the friends *she* chooses, doing the things *they* choose to do...all away from parents. Do you recall the thrill of being away from your parents and hanging out with your friends for the first time? I do, and because my parents were fairly (and perhaps justifiably) overprotective of their only daughter, I felt a sense of freedom and liberation that I had not felt before. The social dynamics of peer groups are such that they offer your teen an opportunity to voice his opinions, express his emotions, and make his decisions (peer groups also provide a context for decision-making skills, all on his own, and this essentially equates to practice. That's right. What I'm suggesting is that by hanging out with his friends, your teen is basically practicing how to be an individual person within the context of a larger social group.

Another behavior that teens get to practice when engaging with peers and peer groups is intimacy. What? Did she just say that my teen will be "practicing intimacy" when hanging out with his friends? In fact, I did. But, when I mention intimacy in this context, I do not mean the "hummuna, hummuna, wink, wink" kind of behavior people typically associate with the word intimacy. What I mean by intimacy is the ability to form close, bonded relationships in which individuals learn to confide and trust in each other, with or without romantic or sexual expectations. These types of deep, meaningful connections aren't typically formed until we reach adolescence, and it is at this developmental period that we begin to build the kinds of friendships that require significant emotional investment, but that are also truly rewarding in both the short and long term. These are the friends that you laugh with, cry with, confide in, trust, and love—and they do the same with you. And again, peer groups provide our teens with the space (and people) to practice making these types of connections.

Romantic connections are not outside the realm of possibility in this context, however, as research has also shown that peer groups assist in helping teens form those types of relationships as well. But before you go into a worry-filled, what-if tailspin as you think about the words *teen* and *sex*, just remember that—much like adolescent distancing is just your teen doing his job in becoming an independent, fully developed person learning to push the proverbial envelope—intimate and even romantic relationships between your teen and those in his peer group are another step in his journey toward becoming a healthy, well-adjusted, mature individual.

Finally, in promoting normal psychosocial development, peers influence one another when it comes to achievement. Teens see others in the group making strides toward goals, and they not only support one another, but individual members learn from other group members about setting goals, working hard, and so on.

It's almost as though achievement becomes contagious, and this is why, although it seems a bit like a roll of the dice, the choices your teen makes regarding the friends or groups of friends she spends time with are critical to her future successes. Of course, the opposite could also be true, where negative examples and negative influences occur. Being part of a group where there *are* no goals or where "achievement" means something other than reaching positive goals—like being the best at skipping school—can be detrimental to your teen's success. In some peer groups studying may be seen as lame and receiving the most Fs is an "honor"!

Even *deviant* peer groups, like gangs for example, involve members forming intimate relationships, supporting one another, and working toward the goals of the group, it's just that the goals do not lie in a direction that is socially recognized as being positive and good. But, recall that we, the parents, play a key role in helping our children to choose the right path from the get-go. The bottom line is that we are assisting our teens as they take on the huge feat of navigating their new social arena and developing into the people that they will ultimately become. Creating a well rounded, socially competent, interesting, and considerate person is essentially a team effort. This is not only a huge responsibility, but it is also very cool, when you think about it. So, the next time your teen asks to go hang out with friends, consider it psychosocial homework, and watch the magic as your teen's individual characteristics develop and flourish.

Social Media

Now let's talk about your teen's social world…online. As you know, social networking has exploded with this generation, and

The Secret Society

these platforms—whether Facebook, Twitter, Instagram, Tumblr, or any number of new sites that may be the latest and coolest by the time this book is on the shelves—are here to stay. In fact, some adults hypothesize (with some amount of fear and trepidation) that, because of the sheer amount of time teens spend on such sites, social networking online is well on its way to replacing face-to-face social interactions with real people. This may be a bit of a stretch, but I fully understand why people think this way. So, how much time are teens spending communicating with their friends online, anyway? What is normal and how much is too much? Is it really possible that my teen has 2,182 *actual friends*, or should we be using quotations around the word "friend" to indicate a new type of relational connection created by this virtual social scene? These are just some of the many questions that parents ask when it comes to their teens' online lives, and, as you may know, a lack of information in this area can create anxiety about who our children are communicating with, what kind of impact online activities have on them and their future, and how can we protect or monitor them, given the fact that we can barely stay ahead of the technological curve, compared with our kids.

Several reports have concluded that an overwhelming majority of adolescents (73 percent) use social networking sites, and they also underscore the massive amounts of time that teens spend on them.[1] I suspect, based on the breakneck speed at which adolescents identify, utilize, and popularize new social media outlets, that the 73 percent figure is actually an underestimate. For example, data from the Kaiser Family Foundation indicate that, on average, eleven- to eighteen-year-olds spend close to eleven hours per day exposed to electronic media.[2] *Eleven hours.* Let's consider this for a moment. Assuming that eight of the twenty-four hours are spent sleeping, that leaves sixteen waking hours—so almost 70 percent of those waking hours are spent in front of some media source. Of course, we know that our teens aren't sitting for eleven consecutive hours immersed in social media. Rather, there is seemingly constant intermittent use via smart phones and other hand-held devices, with teens beginning and ending their day on social media and checking in even in the wee hours of the night when they are supposed to be sleeping. This, together with the endless disruptions to dinners, conversations, and anything else requiring our teens' focus and attention, is the real issue. If none of this sounds familiar to you, then perhaps you are one of the lucky few families whose teen is not entranced by social media; the rest of us should read on.

Why are our teens so completely invested in social media, particularly when they have real, live people they can socialize with, sometimes right in front of them? The answer to this question is multivariate in nature. First and foremost, as both demand for smartphones and Apple's profits indicate, technological devices that access the web in general, and social networking sites in particular, are extremely cool, especially to teens who take great pride in having the latest and greatest in expensive gadgets and other status symbols. Second, adolescents' use of social networking sites has been linked in various studies to important psychosocial constructs, both positive and negative, such as identity formation, popularity and acceptance, autonomy, and development of friendships and peer relationships. The bottom line, though, is that adolescents are all about participating in new trends. This is basically the modern-day equivalent of us, ages ago when we were teens, talking to our friends (using one of those dinosaur landline phones, of course) for hours, not being able to get enough, and having our parents not understand why we felt the need to treat the phone like an extra appendage. Kids today are simply doing what teens do best: socializing. They are vying for position and status in their social world. Building an image. This concept is far from original...we can remember what it was like and how amazingly awesome we were back then!

What *is* new is the way in which this fraternizing is being done, and the space in which it is being conducted. This contemporary version of socializing doesn't involve just one teen talking to another teen. Oh no, my friends. With the help of technology, our children are much more advanced and way more efficient than we used to be when it comes to communicating with friends. Our children are not called "digital natives" for nothing, after all. Because of the countless places they can virtually connect, they can now reach hundreds, if not thousands, of "friends" at once. And they do. Teens today have real power, and they know it. They are well aware of their technological savvy and reach. They are also aware of the fact that they carry a lot of weight when it comes to consumerism and social trends. Adolescents are one of the most sought-after consumer groups in the world, reportedly spending a whopping $250+ billion (yes, that is a *b*!) per year in the United States. Given the technology- and youth-driven society in which we live, teens today are extremely confident in making their web presence known.

Here is the real take-home message about our teens and social media. Our teens live in a very different world than the one in which we were raised. The actual experience of being a teen— wanting to be popular, needing to be liked and accepted, wanting to fit in, and being in complete awe of the surrounding social world—has not changed. What *has* changed, in a big way, is the environment in which all of this is happening. Our teens now have the world quite literally at their fingertips, and when you think about it, this is both tremendously exciting and horrifying at the same time! Our challenge, as parents, is to understand that our teens are just doing what comes naturally to them, and to also understand that they may need some guidance in maneuvering their way through the immense social world they live in. Notice I said guidance, not absolute restriction. I say this because too many parents erroneously think that all they have to do is forbid their teen from using the web, and that will alleviate any worry and solve any anticipated problem. Wrong-O. Regardless of the countless efforts made by online security companies to highlight "parental controls," keeping teens away from the web, and more specifically off social networking sites, is like trying to contain every single grain of sand from entering your pristine house after your family's long day at the beach. Impossible. I recall thinking I was *so* smart when I purposely did not allow computers in my teens' rooms, but instead set up the family computer in the kitchen, where we all had full view of any potential online shenanigans. Of course, that little pearl of wisdom went out the window when smart phones took over and kids gained access to the web any-where, anytime. We, as parents, are better off communicating with our teens about their online whereabouts and letting them know you are there for help, guidance, and support. Here are a few tips to consider when it comes to your teen and the Internet:

- Understand and appreciate that your teen's access to the web is virtually limitless, and her desire (need, really) to be part of that new-world social scene is just as immense.
- Also know that social networking sites are not going any-where, so it is wise to consider the "if you can't beat 'em,

join 'em" attitude that so many parents adopt. I suggest that you get with the program and create an online presence yourself. This way, you might (1) see what all the fuss is about; and (2) secretly spy on your kid's virtual activities!

- Instead of putting energy into futile efforts to keep teens off of the web/social networking sites all together, parents should ask for *and* give respect. What I mean is, we as parents should respect the fact that our teen's web presence and social interactions are important to him; similarly, ask that he respect the boundaries you, as the parent, set regarding the amount of time he can spend online and the type of web-based activities you will allow.
- Have a discussion with your teen about the advantages, disadvantages, and possible dangers that the web and social media sites offer, and then, together, decide what is reasonable when it comes to boundaries.
- Periodically (in a casual way...no lectures, please) check in with your teen about social networking sites. Ask, "How many friends do you have? Anybody new or interesting?" Ask how things are going, just as if this online social scene is the equivalent of hanging out with friends at a real place after school.

There you have it, a bit of insight into the black hole that is your teen's social world. Teens like social interaction, but you already knew this. They want to form strong peer relationships, and my guess is that you already knew this too. What you may not know is that teens with poor peer relationships are more likely to be low achievers in school, drop out of high school, show higher rates of delinquent behavior, and suffer from emotional and mental health problems as adults. What this means is that our teens' social world (yes, even online) is vital to their overall psychosocial health and well-being. So we all benefit when we inform ourselves and support our teens in every way possible. Your teen may not show it (mine hardly ever does), but he will love you for it!

7

Love

Teen Dating, Romantic Relationships, and...the "S Word"

Ah, love. The stuff that makes the world go 'round, leaves us swooning, and creates that feeling of walking on air with butter-flies in our bellies, barely able to catch our breath. Also the stuff that makes us want to pull our hair out, scream at the top of our lungs, and declare all-out emotional warfare. Love, despite its ups, downs, and unpredictability, is something we're all after. Young, old, male, female, gay, straight...when we are asked about our greatest hope or goal in life, our response usually centers around obtaining a stable and loving relationship with a romantic part-ner.[1] In fact, love is such an important construct that researchers have studied it for years, investigating the different types, taxono-mies, and styles, as well as how to keep it once you've finally found that elusive and magical potion. But what I want to explore in this chapter is that transformation from the loving bonds we share with our parents and family to the passionate union we seek in a romantic partner, and which we seemingly need for survival as individuals and as a species.

What is love, anyway? The word is tossed around, overused, misused, quoted, and commercialized so much that it's difficult to determine what it really means. Certainly, the context in which we consider this emotion matters: I love to read; I love Chinese food; I love my mother. To be clear, I am interested in how we develop and pursue the takes-my-breath-away, euphoric, romantic love that is so sought after. My two daughters and I were watching a movie the other night called *Wedding Crashers* (we're all suckers for rom-coms), and we heard Owen Wilson say, "True love is the soul's recognition of its counterpoint in another"...sigh. The *Merriam-Webster Dictionary* lists various definitions: "a feeling of strong or constant affection for a person"; "attraction that includes sexual desire"; and "the strong affection felt by people who have a romantic relationship." But do any of these descriptions really answer our question?

As children, we experience love in the form of unconditional care and affection from our parents. That is indeed love, but does that concept somehow shift as we get older? When we become teens, is one form replaced by another, or is it the same construct on some blissfully complicated continuum? Some researchers have argued that the "targets" of our intimacy change over time, so that intimacy with peers replaces intimacy with parents, and intimacy with peers of the opposite sex replaces intimacy with same-sex friends.[2]

There are two problems with this line of reasoning: first, the terms *intimacy* and *love*, despite much overlap, are not the same thing and should not be used interchangeably. Romantic love is basically intimacy with the added bonus of sexual attraction and passionate commitment—the beautiful sexual icing on the delicious intimacy cake, if you will. Second, most researchers contend that, instead of anyone being replaced or made unimportant, as we get older and expand our social network, new targets of intimacy and affection are added to old ones. I propose that the same thing happens with love. Not only does our concept and understanding of love shift from that which we feel for our parents, siblings, dogs, and so on to a richer and deeper feeling for another person outside our familial circle, but it also cumulatively adds to the concept of love that we began with. This is why so many people exclaim, "I never knew love could be *so*...amazing, deep, fulfilling, complicated, exhausting..." You get the picture.

Dating

Before we continue with how romantic love develops in adolescence, let's consider dating. I realize that many parents labor over if and when to allow their teen to begin dating. I clearly recall, when I began to show interest in dating boys, my father saying something about putting me into a convent until I was thirty! But again, because I truly believe that knowledge is power, I would like to offer some historical perspective, so as to alleviate any angst over your little girl or little boy going out with some kid you don't know or trust. In past generations, dating in high school or college, for at least some, served a very specific function: mate selection. That was certainly the case for many in previous cohorts of college women seeking what was so optimistically termed an "MRS. degree." Offended? Don't shoot the messenger: I'm simply relaying historical factoids. Because marriage today, if it occurs at all, is happening much later in life (the average age is around twenty-seven for women and twenty-nine for men)[3] dating for high school students has now taken on an entirely new meaning.

In today's world, dating in adolescence no longer holds the sole purpose of mate selection; rather, it has become an introduction to the world of intimacy, relationship roles, sexual experimentation, and, yes, romantic love. It's almost like practice for the real thing that is yet to come. And despite the fact that high school dating for today's teenagers has little to do with long-term commitments and/or marriage, modern-day romantic relationships among teens are very common, with approximately one-fourth of twelve-year olds, one-half of fifteen-year olds, and more than two-thirds of eighteen-year olds reporting being in a romantic, dating relationship in the past eighteen months.[4]

To help you put things in perspective (i.e., is the age at which my teen begins dating normal?), on average here in the U.S. teens begin dating around the age of thirteen, and by the age of sixteen more than 90 percent of teens have had at least one date.[5] And finally, the average duration of romantic relationships in high school is about six months. Some of you will read this and think, "Dating? My baby? At twelve?" That thought will quickly be followed by a sense of dread that feels like someone unexpectedly delivered a hard, swift kick right to your gut. But let's think about this: when we contemplate teens dating at twelve, or perhaps even fourteen years of age, what we must realistically consider is what dating means at that age. What are they really doing?

Most often, dating during early adolescence involves exchanging contact information (i.e., giving cell phone numbers for texting, becoming friends or followers on social networking sites); engaging in harmless communication via text and SMSs; seeing each other at school; and maybe even holding hands as they walk through the halls, displaying their "couplehood" so that peer onlookers can eat their hearts out with envy. It's a social status thing. By the age of fifteen or sixteen, teens move toward qualitatively different and more meaningful romantic relationships; certainly, by the time they are seventeen or eighteen, they begin to think about their romantic relationships in a much deeper, more mature, and long-term way, with significant growth in both emotional and physical interests and commitment. These older adolescents tend to form more adultlike versions of romantic love and attachment, and stay in relationships that last over a year, on average. This is, whether we like it or not, when things get real.

You recall me stating earlier that dating during the teen years serves as a type of practice for future relationships? In fact, in addition to helping to develop intimacy with others, dating serves many purposes for our teens. This is good news, really. Despite our reluctance and fear that our "babies" are venturing into the big scary world of dating, love, and sex, (most certainly to get their hearts shattered into a million pieces), by allowing our teens to date, we are actually helping them to become healthy, mature, informed individuals who are training to be good relational partners. Dating not only helps teens establish emotional and behavioral autonomy from their parents, it also furthers their development of gender identity, helps them learn about themselves and their own role as a romantic partner, and establishes social status and perhaps even popularity in their peer groups.

Having said all this, I should note that there are a couple of potential pitfalls when it comes to teens in the context of romantic relationships. First, studies have shown that early and intensive (exclusive and serious) dating before the age of fifteen can have a somewhat stunting effect on adolescents' psychosocial development. By getting involved in serious relationships, spending virtually all their time with only one person, teens can run the risk of missing out on other types of social interactions (building other types of relationships, practicing intimacy, gaining different perspectives, and simply having fun with other friends!). This can prove limiting to them in terms of achieving their full potential of psychosocial growth and development. Conversely, research has also shown that adolescent girls, specifically, who do not date at all may tend toward underdeveloped social skills, excessive dependency on their parents, and feelings of insecurity when it comes to meeting romantic interests or potential partners.

In sum, allowing our teens to date and explore romantic relationships (in moderation) is a good thing. So, the next time you cringe at the prospect of your teen dating and possibly even becoming romantically involved with another teen, remember that it is yet another way for him to grow and develop into the well-rounded, caring person you want him to be, particularly in the context of long-term, loving relationships.

Love, and Making It Last

Now, let's return our focus to the concept of love. As adults, we assume that teens know absolutely nothing about this complicated and wondrous emotion. We think that all they experience in those early relationships is immature infatuation, and that the genuine, all-encompassing, deep, and passionate love that we experience is somehow reserved for adults. While some of these assumptions may be warranted, we should also consider that perhaps our teens deserve a bit more credit. Do you recall the first time you thought you were in love? I do. I was in high school, and I was certain, beyond any shadow of a doubt, that the emotions that washed over me every minute of every day were in fact true love. And perhaps they were, because I have to tell you, I have never felt anything quite like that euphoric teen love since. Love is a rare and elusive thing to many (young and old), and despite all our meditations on the subject, none of us really has the answer to the myriad questions that surround it. Enter researcher and renowned relationship expert John Gottman, coauthor of many books on relationship successes and failures.[5]

Gottman has made an entire career of investigating what makes relationships work and what makes them fail by studying thousands (tens of thousands, if you can believe it) of couples in his "Love Lab." This guy is so good, in fact, that he can predict with over 90 percent accuracy which couples in his studies will divorce or separate and which will stay together and be happy. Gottman categorizes couples (heterosexual and gay or lesbian, older and younger) into what he calls "Masters" (those who stay together and still like each other) and "Disasters" (those who break up or stay together, but are miserable). The larger goal of this research, of course, is to inform the masses of people searching for long-lasting love about what to do and what to avoid to make a relationship work. Why do I bring this up in the context of adolescence and the development of romantic love? The answer is fairly simple. If our goal, as parents of teens, is to teach and/or guide our children in ways that will help them become self-sufficient, happy, healthy, and well-informed adults, then why not teach them how to succeed in their quest for a loving relationship? At minimum, this is good information for us all to keep in our back pockets—and perhaps our own relationships will benefit from it as well! So, here are some of the main findings from Gottman's Love Lab:

What do the Disasters do? Gottman calls the following behaviors the Four Horsemen of the Apocalypse. Behaviors to avoid:

- **Criticism:** Finger-pointing; looking for the bad; "I'm perfect and you are an idiot…"
- **Defensiveness:** Warding off the perceived attack from partner and launching a counterattack; also acting like an innocent victim; "Oh yeah, well…you suck in bed!"
- **Contempt:** This is the best predictor of breakups; insulting partner; feeling like you are better/above your partner; holding something over him/her; "You're an idiot, what you're saying is ridiculous…"
- **Stonewalling:** Shutting down; not giving the usual signals that a listener gives a speaker.

What do the *Masters* do? Behaviors to embrace:

- **Good communication:** When faced with conflict in a relationship (and we all are at some time), talk about feelings and needs…and allow your partner to do the same.
- **Appreciation:** Build a culture of appreciation and respect by paying attention to the small moments; "You're such a good person, I admire you"; small things often make a big difference.
- **Engagement:** Masters may want to stonewall, but instead they breathe, calm down, and stay connected.
- **Positive attitude:** Masters say five positive things for every negative thing; Disasters say .8 (not even one!) positive thing for every negative thing. Disasters try to balance, but

Masters are saying far more positive things than negative things.

Truly happy couples:

- Know little things about one another and build shared meanings
- Share fondness, admiration, and respect
- Continue to communicate with positive perspective
- Ask about partner's thoughts, dreams, goals
- Have a satisfying, healthy sex life
- Have built a solid foundation of trust and loyalty
- Laugh—a lot
- Are good friends!

Sex

Now, let's talk about sex. We've already discussed how to approach this tough topic when preparing to have conversations with your teen, back in chapter 5. Now it's time to consider sexuality as a developmental issue and, more importantly, as an adolescent issue, and to think about how it can potentially impact our own teens. We are all sexual beings, and regardless of our respective religious backgrounds or moral belief systems, we, as parents of teens, should be informed about sexuality as it relates to our children. In fact, we owe it to our teens to be open to learning about the experiences they will go through, and to accept that sexual development is a normal and healthy part of becoming an adult. If we can talk and listen without judgment or ridicule, we can show our teens that we are a dependable and informed resource for them.

As children, we may be curious about our bodies, and we may even begin to realize that certain body parts simply feel good when touched. This is a very basic, physiological reaction, and children don't read too much into the meanings or implications of this fact. After puberty, however, teens experience significant changes in the nature and meaning of sexual behavior. Because of the physical, cognitive, and social changes that have occurred in our emerging teens, our newly minted adolescents now see and experience interactions with other teens very differently. In the physical realm, puberty has set off a chain of reactions, including a surge of sex hormones that not only trigger physical development but also awaken a newfound interest in and physical attraction to the opposite sex (or same sex, as the case may be). And, of course, postpubertal sexual activity can lead to pregnancy, which none of us likes to think about when pondering our own teen's physical development and sexual behavior. It is a fact, nonetheless. Again, please don't shoot the messenger!

In the cognitive domain, teens now have the capacity to be very introspective and reflective about sex and sexual behavior, what it means in society, what is expected of them, how they, as individuals, feel about it, and how to reconcile this information with the new physical feelings and urges they are experiencing. It can be terrifying, exciting, and confusing all at the same time for our teens. Sadly, sexual topics can also cause embarrassment and shame, given the fact that we, as a society, tend to give the message that sex before marriage is immoral and that if something feels really good (physically), it is usually bad. By the way, it should be noted that we also bombard our teens—via ads, billboards, magazine images, Internet pop-ups, and so on—with the idea that sex is not only good, but that sex and drinking are glamorous and off-the-chain fantastic! These mixed messages that teens receive hundreds of times a day clearly add to the confusion.

In the teen social world, sex is more visible, more acceptable, and more available, given the opportunities afforded teens in their social contexts. Teens are now spending more time with friends, often of the opposite sex, and are often unsupervised by parents or other adults, so yes, opportunities arise. They are now also much better at reading social cues and nonverbal messages like the look from across the room that says, "Hey, I like you...I mean, I *really* like you (wink, wink)...are you interested?" Is this our cue to lock up our teens and never allow them to spend unsupervised time alone with a girlfriend/boyfriend? Clearly not, because as we all know (likely from our own experiences), if we draw a line in the sand and make definitive statements like, "You are absolutely *not* allowed to see that boy, especially alone...." Let's just say we'd be asking for the much-dreaded teenage rebellion.

If you haven't already put the book down in complete horror, I thank you for sticking with me. I realize that this is one of the most difficult topics that parents have to deal with when it comes to their children, but know that I am right there with you. It's tough, but informing ourselves is not only good for us as parents (more informational tools for the conversational toolbox), it is most definitely beneficial for our teens. To that end, I would like to present you with some background and context on what teens are actually doing when it comes to sexual activity. But first, some good news: despite media portrayals, which cause our fears and imaginations to run wild, sexual promiscuity in adolescence is rare. I can hear the collective sigh of relief now. With this fact in mind, let us proceed.

Most of us begin our sexual explorations and activity in stages. The first stage is engaging in what scientists and researchers call autoerotic behavior. That is, sexual behavior that is experienced alone (e.g., having erotic fantasies, masturbation, nocturnal orgasms). As our teens reach high school, they typically begin an orderly progression to sexual activity involving another person. Interestingly, because most people tend to believe that boys and men corner the proverbial market on masturbation, they also believe that only boys go through these stages of sexual activity. Not so. Various studies have shown that both males and females engage in a very similar sequence; it's just that boys engage in these activities at a somewhat earlier age than girls do. Here is another piece of good news, parents: in terms of prevalence of sexual intercourse among teens, slightly fewer adolescents are having sex today when we compare them with teens in previous decades. Having said this, the reality we must all face is that sexual intercourse during high school is now a part of the normative experience of adolescence in America. A bit scary, but true. And this is precisely why we need to arm our teens with knowledge and information—we want them to make smart and informed decisions when it comes to sex.

One of the lines of research I find absolutely fascinating is the timing of sexual initiation (i.e., when youngsters lose their virginity). Various findings indicate that teenagers are more likely to lose their virginity at certain times of the year, particularly during early summer or over the Christmas holidays. More specifically, December (the holiday season) is peak time for teens to engage in sex for the first time, especially when they are involved in a serious relationship. Conversely, the months of May, June, and July are common, regardless of whether teens are romantically involved with another person or not. "Why does this occur?" you may ask. Let's think about it. During the summer months, it is hot, people are at the beach, pool, etc., wearing considerably less clothing, and events like prom and graduation are happening, followed by kids going off to college at the end of the summer. During the month of December, couples are swept up by the sentimentality and romanticism that surrounds the holiday season—in addition, they are both giving and receiving meaningful gifts and gestures. So, interestingly, the timing of first sexual activities can have some predictability—you have now been armed with that knowledge, and may do with it what you will. My suggestion: if you know that your teen son or daughter is dating or romantically involved with another youngster, you may consider having a heart-to-heart conversation with him or her around these key times, so you can answer any questions and provide guidance. Another area of investigation concerns gender differences concerning the meaning placed on having sex. I may be stating the obvious when I say that, when it comes to the meaning of sex, boys and girls experience and interpret sex very differently. This is where the whole *Men Are from Mars, Women Are from Venus* thinking comes into play. Teen boys are likely to keep matters of intimacy (bonding, sharing, closeness, trust) separate from matters of sex when compared with teen girls. According to researcher Larry Steinberg, adolescent boys are more likely to interpret intercourse in terms of recreation than intimacy, whereas adolescent girls tend to integrate intimacy, emotional involvement, romance, love, and friendship into sexual activity.[6] My intention is not to place blame or judgment on the male gender (I have three brothers and two sons, myself), but rather to point out that, whether it's because of social influences or biological hard wiring, men and women are simply different when it comes to interpreting sexual experiences. Of course, this is not to say that young men are incapable of incorporating intimacy and love into sexual encounters; nor am I insinuating that young women can't separate emotions from sexual behaviors, but the vast majority of those studied fall into the stated trends.

Finally, despite trends that show adolescent sexual activity decreasing slightly since 1995, one-third of teens still have early sexual intercourse (before ninth grade). It is also important to note that early sexual activity, involving teens aged fifteen years or younger, has been associated with a number of other variables such as experimentation with drugs and alcohol, lower levels of religious involvement, minor delinquency, lower interest in academic achievement, and stronger orientation toward independence. A strong word of caution in interpreting these findings, however: researchers found an association (correlation), which is not to say that one variable causes the other but rather that the variables are likely somehow related. Another critical point to stress is that sexual activity during later adolescence (age sixteen or older) is not associated with any sort of psychological disturbance, and levels of self-esteem and life satisfaction are on par with those of the overall adolescent population.

The Good News

I realize that all of this talk about our teens having sex is daunting and somewhat intimidating. But as a parent myself, I think the subject also leads us to wonder whether we have any influence over our teens' involvement in sexual activity or if teen sex is some inevitable, foregone conclusion. In response, I offer you yet one more piece of good news. I've said this before, and I will say it again: parents can make a big difference! When it comes to parenting styles and practices, authoritative parenting—an approach in which parents communicate regularly with their children, hold high expectations and standards, engage in give-and-take conversations when making decisions, and are firm yet loving and supportive—has been associated with teens who are less likely to become sexually active at an early age and less likely to engage in risky sexual activity. Talking (and listening) to your teen about sex is indeed important, and although it may not prevent them from being sexually active in general, it definitely stops them from engaging in risky sexual behaviors, which should put our minds at ease at least a bit. So take heed, my friends.

Ann Landers once pointed out that "Love is friendship that has caught fire." As social creatures, we all seek close personal connections. These start in childhood as we participate in weekly playdates, and we gain more experience with intimacy as we find the high school best friend or first love we thought would last forever; as we mature, we learn to cultivate those connections that will endure. We are all driven by the need for social interaction, but contrary to what some may think, it does not happen by chance or by magic. As children, and later as teens, we go through a developmental process to reach the ultimate goal of deep social connection, and when we do, the rewards are endless. When our teens spend time with friends, explore social networking sites, take a chance on love, and even as they discover the perilous joys of sexuality, they are becoming grown-ups in the social world. And we parents are the lucky ones who get to help them on this beautiful journey of self-discovery. What could be better than that?

8

Problems in Adolescence

Being Aware of Potential Pitfalls

When we think of the potential problems that can occur in adolescence, we typically fall back on media portrayals of the stereotypical teenager. You know what I mean: words like angst, dark, sullen, rebellious, thug, hoodlum, and even criminal come to mind. The stereotypical teen pushes legal limits and fights social norms. This teen makes parents cringe and teachers furious, and, worse yet, makes other teens gaze in awe and amazement at the sheer guts it takes to shoot the proverbial bird at everything approved in our boring, lame, adult-run society. But is this an accurate portrayal of teens today? Is there something to be said for such stereotypes, or are we simply watching out for the wrong things? In this chapter, I'll discuss the real problems adolescents face today. Despite exaggerations and hyperbolic representations of teens in movies, ads, memes, and the like, adolescents today really do face some serious issues that we, as parents, should be aware of. Of course, we are all cognizant of the possibilities involving drugs and alcohol, because we were young once too. But in addition to substance use, depression, eating attitudes and disorders, and, most salient to teens today, stress are all areas of vulnerability for teens.

By now, you've certainly realized that, yes, our teens like to push limits and question authority, and they take an "us versus them" attitude when it comes to adult expectations and societal standards. But let me begin this chapter on a positive note. Contrary to the image of teens the media depicts and the stereotypes we carry in our own minds, most adolescents do not develop serious social or psychological problems, nor are they doomed to a life of crime and orange jumpsuits. Whew! That's a relief. Most of the problems experienced by teens today reflect transitory experimentation in adolescence rather than enduring patterns of bad behavior.[1]

For most kids, the problems they confront or the trouble they get into during their teen years have to do with (and are mostly limited to) what is happening during that particular point in time (for example, adolescent peer pressure, social rebellion, getting a girl's attention . . .) and are not necessarily predictive of a negative future outcome. Most will end up as well-adjusted, productive, law-abiding citizens. This is basically the "teens will be teens" argument. To make this point, every semester I say to my students in my Adolescent Psychology class: "Raise your hand if you ever did anything really stupid when you were a teenager that could have possibly landed you in trouble with the law or put you in some sort of danger." At first, only a few hands go up. Then, after several quick glances around the room, some nonjudgmental encouragement from me, and a few snickers and nervous laughs, virtually every student's hand ends up in the air. Bottom line: we all push limits when we're teens, but as we grow older, and presumably more mature and responsible, we tend to let go of the rebellious streak and become the boring, socially conforming adults our children know and love.

It should be noted that, although most problems (such as drug and alcohol use, unemployment, and delinquency) experienced during adolescence do not persist into adulthood, when troubles do occur, they don't necessarily begin in adolescence. In fact, some—whether they are genetically based predispositions (as toward substance use/abuse) or environmentally influenced (like the type of parenting a child receives)—have their roots in childhood. Another important point to remember is that problems during adolescence are not caused by adolescence itself. That is, simply being a teenager and going through that tough transitional period is not the origin or cause of anything that goes wrong. So, despite what we hear, "raging hormones" do not cause problem behaviors.

Let us now turn our focus to the things that *can* go wrong during adolescence. When we psychologists study teen behavior, we tend to do a lot of categorizing. Serious problems in adolescence are generally lumped into two categories: internalizing and externalizing disorders (with the term "disorders" used very loosely). Internalizing disorders can occur when problems or serious concerns are turned *inward*, and teens experience emotional and cognitive distress. Examples of internalizing disorders are adolescent depression, anxiety, and eating disorders. Conversely, externalizing disorders can occur when teens turn their problems *outward*, which generally results in behavioral problems of some sort. Examples are substance use/abuse, conduct problems in school, and trouble with the law. Because of the importance of these issues for many people, we'll tackle externalizing problems, and specifically substance use in adolescence, first.

Substance Use

Through their use of smartphones, tablets, televisions, and other devices, teens today are constantly bombarded with mixed messages when it comes to drugs and alcohol. In the United States, in particular, we send conflicting messages to teens almost continually, via our efficient, effective, immediate, and insanely powerful media outlets. What are these messages? On the one hand, you have the "Just say no" directive. This message takes the form of television and radio commercials, magazine and pop-up ads, and billboards and signs in schools, and it has even been spotlighted in several political campaigns, all in an effort to get kids to just say no to drugs and alcohol. You remember these, don't you? My favorite is still the one that goes something like this: "This is your brain." (Scene: man holding an egg in his hand.) "This is your brain on drugs." (Man cracks egg into skillet, and it immediately fries like, well, like a fried egg!) The host concludes his lesson with a daring, "Any questions?" Classic. Regardless of how effective or ineffective these ads are (more on that later in the chapter), this message is pretty clear: using drugs or consuming alcohol is bad....*Don't do it, kids!*

But here is where the "mixed" part of mixed message comes into play. The other unspoken message that teens get, pretty much all the time, is that drugs and alcohol are *fun*. They are cool. And if you want to be beautiful, rich, surrounded by lots of gorgeous friends, and have tons of sexy people want to be near you, then all you (teens) have to do is drink this particular drink or take this particular drug. Sound like a cynical, or perhaps even conspiratorial, exaggeration? Take a close look at ads that teens are regularly exposed to, whether the ads are on TV, on the web, or in magazines (for example: a picture showing a hot rapper holding a certain brand of gin), and you'll start to notice that advertisers never show the sad reality behind what drugs and alcohol can do to a person. This is no accident. When faced with these mixed messages, teens end up feeling confused and frustrated, and they begin to question who to believe: old people wagging their finger and saying, "Just say no," or the fun, sexy crowd? My money is on the sexy people.

Does this mean that all teens are behaving like social deviants, as the stereotypes suggest, by doing tons of drugs and alcohol? The answer is a resounding no, but I beg you to resist the temptation to offer up the knee-jerk reaction that many parents give: "Oh, not *my* son...he would never..."; "God, no, not *my* daughter, she knows better...." Rather, let's consider research-based facts. According to Monitoring the Future data,[2] alcohol and cigarettes are by far the most commonly used and abused substances. In fact, research shows that a large percentage of adolescents have experimented with alcohol, tobacco, and marijuana, with 70 percent of high school seniors having tried alcohol, 46 percent having smoked marijuana, and 40 percent having smoked cigarettes. And please note that, because these data are based on self-reports, they are probably serious *under*estimates—the real numbers are likely much higher.

The upside to this scenario is that, although a significant proportion of teens have at least tried these substances, only a small percentage (approximately 9 percent) reported experimenting with any other type of more serious illicit drugs. Although it may not seem like it, this *is* good news, folks. What does this have to do with *my* teen, you may ask? My response, very similar to my comments on teen sexuality, is that we parents need to be realistic and honest with ourselves when it comes to the possibility that our teens may indeed be drinking alcohol or experimenting with other substances (remember our discussion on adolescent risk taking?). Again, we should talk to our children. We need to communicate with them early and often about what's going on in the big, scary world; about our expectations and concerns; about their curiosity and interests; their friends; and about our love, concern, and commitment to them. In fact, early communication between parents and teens about drugs and alcohol is critical, because we know that the chances of a person becoming addicted to alcohol or nicotine increase when use begins before age fifteen. Further, despite the fact that experimentation with drugs is less common among younger teens now than it has been in the past, we also know that the long-term effects of drug and alcohol use on brain functioning are more severe when use begins in adolescence versus adulthood. Because of these admittedly scary statistics, it is important for us, as parents of teens, to keep in mind that marketers and advertisers are "catching" our children early by exposing them to ads from the time they are born. (This is precisely why I get both angry and sad when I see a toddler with his or her very own iPad at the dinner table!) We need to beat them to the proverbial punch by arming our children with facts very early on, to help them be aware and make informed, and hopefully smart, decisions when they are offered booze or drugs at a high school party or another social situation.

Risk and Protective Factors

Why do some teens get into real trouble, while others escape when it comes to drugs and alcohol? This can be explained, at least in part, by examining the risk and protective factors that may predispose or prevent teens from falling prey to substance use. First, the risk factors: one of the variables that may put some teens at risk for drug and alcohol use and abuse is *personality*. Teens who have a lot of unresolved anger issues, display impulsive behaviors, and are inattentive and can't stay focused are at risk. Another risk factor is the *social environment* in which teens spend their time. When they spend time with friends who either use or tolerate the use of drugs, and/or if they live in a context that makes drug use easy because drugs are easily available, teens are at risk. The last major risk factor lies within the *family*. When teens are part of a dysfunctional family situation, where all they have to turn to are distant, hostile, or conflictual relationships, they are at risk. As you can surmise, any of these variables alone is less than ideal, but the factors may also have cumulative effects, as many teens experience two or more of these risk factors, resulting in multiplicative negative results.

Now for the protective factors: adolescents who experience *positive mental health*, who are actively *engaged in school* and achieve *high academic successes*, have close and *supportive family relationships* and/or mentorships, and are *involved in community and/or religious activities* are at significantly lower risk for substance use and abuse. Clearly, the more protective factors a young person has, the better. And, most salient to us, as parents of teens, is the role of family and friends in helping teens feel supported and loved. Having a relationship with your teen that includes open and honest communication, as well as firm but reasonable expectations, is key.

Unlike the many preventative programs that primarily rely on ads and scare tactics, and that have tried and failed to keep teens off drugs by pouring millions of governmental dollars into efforts such as the Just Say No or D.A.R.E. campaigns (the likes of which, teens find quite entertaining, but do not take seriously), the factors that most positively impact our teens are those that they experience in their daily lives. These big programs fail for various reasons, including the fact that teens can't relate to them and simply don't take them seriously. Most experts believe that it is more realistic to focus prevention efforts on teens' specific motivations and their own environment. In other words, what works is tapping into what teens care about and where they spend their time—so it really does "take a village" to overcome the romanticized images surrounding drugs and alcohol that come through the media machine every day, but it can be done, and it starts with you!

We must remember: our teens are young, adventurous, and curious, and they want to push the limits and have a little fun—or maybe *a lot* of fun. As parents, we should be vigilant in warning our teens of the dangers involved in alcohol and drug use, and of course we should set standards and expectations, but we should also take care not to act in such a way that we make these illicit substances another of those "forbidden fruits" that we absolutely prohibit yet end up actually pushing our teens toward. It's scary as hell, I know, and not the easiest job to walk that line, but this is why my mother always says, "Parenting is not for cowards." So I encourage you to stay informed, stay strong, and stay engaged.

Depression

Switching gears to the internalizing issues that adolescents experience all too frequently, we will tackle the topic of depression first. I should begin by saying that, in this necessarily brief coverage of the topic, we will not be able to fully address the range of causes and treatment of depression in adolescence. It is my intention, rather, to give you, as parents of teens, some insight into the dark world that so many young people experience, as well as some signs to watch out for in your own teen.

Depression is characterized by a pervasive unhappy mood that is significantly more severe than the occasional blues or mood swings everyone gets from time to time.[3] Without getting too bogged down with clinical or psychiatric terminology, I want to make clear that depression in this context goes beyond the typical sadness that people experience in reaction to stress, difficult life events, or even the loss of a loved one, although these events can trigger clinical depression; instead, it is the type of sadness that causes people to feel hopeless and helpless, though they have no real, justifiable explanation for why they are feeling so devastated.

Children and teens who suffer with depression can't shake this debilitating feeling of despair, and it becomes so pervasive that it interferes with daily routines, social relationships, school performance, and overall functioning. And, because they can't fully comprehend or explain why they are feeling this way, depression experienced by teens is often accompanied by anxiety and acting out (i.e., conduct problems), and therefore often goes unrecognized and untreated. In fact, one of the most difficult things for us to do as parents is to tease apart how much of our teens' sullen, brooding, and angst-filled behavior is normal, moody teenage stuff and how much of it is something we should be concerned about. It's difficult, to be sure, especially if you're new to the parenting teens game.

Sadly, depression is the most common psychological disturbance among adolescents, and interestingly is significantly more common in teen girls (after puberty) than teen boys. Some of these reasons include higher societal pressures and expectations for girls, in addition to higher incidents of peer pressure and internalizing behaviors among girls when compared to boys. The symptoms for depression are categorized into four different types: the *emotional* symptoms include low self-esteem, gloominess, and feelings of hopelessness, helplessness, and worthlessness. Teens with depression tend to feel that no matter what they do or how hard they try, nothing they do will make a difference. They may also experience loss of enjoyment or pleasure in things they enjoyed immensely before becoming depressed (i.e. friends, food, even sex).

The *cognitive* symptoms include pessimism and invasive negative thoughts and interpretations. Teens have a hard time seeing the positive aspects of anything when in the depths of depression. *Motivational* symptoms can take the form of apathy and boredom. As you may imagine, because these are two behaviors we are used to seeing in nondepressed teens, it is difficult to think about them in the context of depression. But depressed teens truly give up. They feel as though there is no reason to continue trying, fighting, or even sometimes living, and it is this deep despair that is so frightening to see in young people suffering with this condition. Finally, the *physical* symptoms can include fluctuation in appetite (sometimes a total loss of appetite, other times eating to try to make oneself feel better), difficulty sleeping (or, in some cases, sleeping all the time or not being able to get out of bed), and loss of energy.

Depression is an equal opportunity disorder. Although the rates for teen girls are considerably higher than for teen boys, depression does not discriminate, and can affect a teen regardless of gender, social background, income, or achievement level. Regarding ethnicity, demographic statistics from the U.S. Census Bureau and Center for Disease Control (CDC) (2014)[4] show Latino teens having slightly higher rates of depression (6.3 percent) than African American teens (6 percent), and even higher than Caucasian teens (4.8 percent). Teens living below the poverty line in the United States experience dramatically higher depression rates (13.1 percent) when compared to teens at or above the poverty level. And, with respect to gender, before adolescence males are slightly more likely to exhibit depressive symptoms, but after puberty teen girls are significantly more likely to experience depression.

What do all these statistics mean? Which teens are at risk and how can we help? Clearly, the numbers from the CDC indicate that living in poverty makes life extremely difficult for some teens, which can present individuals with a multitude of problems and stressors. And something about the experience of being a minority (by ethnicity or gender) in this country—confronting daily challenges and constant stressors—also makes some adolescents more prone to depression. But the issue of why some teens struggle with depression, while others in similar situations do not, is still a mystery.

Enter, the nature versus nurture debate. Despite the fact that some scientists and researchers still argue that biology and genetics have more influence, and some counter that the environment in which we live plays a stronger role in developmental outcomes, it's no longer a debate, really. Most experts agree that *both* biological *and* environmental factors are vital when searching for answers about depression and other psychological conditions that affect so many young people. In the case of depression, it is the adolescent who has a genetic predisposition (a family history, with a mother or father who has or had depression) *and* some form of severe life stressor (such as poverty, conflict in the family, discrimination, etc.) who is most at risk for experiencing depression. Another difficult thing for us to do is to understand the fact that what teens may consider a "severe" stressor may not be interpreted in the same way by adults; but severity is a relative term, and it is our teens' interpretations of this negative impact that matter most when it comes to their feelings of depression.

What other factors can put teens at risk for depression? Other risk factors that increase the chances of teen depression include: previous episodes of depression, experiences of trauma or abuse, and additional untreated problems such as other mental disorders, anxiety, or addiction to drugs or alcohol. As with substance use, the more risk factors that an adolescent experiences, the more likely it is that he will succumb to depression, especially if he has a family history of the disorder.

I should note that not all teens who experience depression do so to the same extent. Some experience mild cases of depression, that, with the right treatment strategy, seem fairly manageable, while others plunge into such deep depression that, despite treatment and intervention, they see no way out. Immensely troubling is the fact that approximately 20 percent of girls and 10 percent of boys think about killing themselves (suicidal ideation; annual percentages), and 10 percent of girls and 6 percent of boys make attempts serious enough to require treatment. Suicide is so devastatingly frightening to parents that most of us would rather not even think of it. Of course, it is completely understandable that we would want to bury our heads in the sand and deny the fact that some teens become so depressed that they actually think of ending their own lives. But the sad reality is that it is happening, and we must arm ourselves with information so that we can spot warning signs in our own children.

There are strategies and resources specifically meant to help families in dealing with depression. And, given the fact that the rates of depression among U.S. teens are so high (especially among teen girls), we must each seek out those resources and do what is right for *our* family, *our* teen. Despite what many may think, there is no one solution that works for everyone. Some families seek therapeutic interventions (i.e., family, individual, or group therapies) to help adolescents understand the roots of their depression and change their thought processes, or help families change patterns of relationships that may contribute to symptoms; others explore more biological approaches, such as antidepressant medications (SSRIs) that address the neuroendocrine problems that may exist. Many families find that a combination of therapy *and* medication provides the best solution for their teen. It all depends on what works for *your* child and *your* family.

One thing we do know for sure is that, due to pressures around school, work, families, relationships, social media, and the seemingly endless series of transitions involved in simply being an adolescent, teens today are under more stress than ever before. Being a teenager, especially in today's world, is hard; and, of course, parenting a teen may be just as hard. To that end, I'd like to end this section on a more positive note: if you are a parent of a teen struggling with depression, know that you are not alone. Numerous families are fighting similar battles, and there are several online communities and support groups specifically focused on helping teens with depression. Use these resources to help decide what treatment strategy will work best for you. If, on the other hand, you have not had firsthand experience with teen depression, consider yourself blessed and informed. Here are some warning signs to look out for:

- Does your child want to spend significantly more time alone—compared to previous times, when he would rather spend time with friends or family?
- Have you seen any obvious decreases in activities or interests that your teen used to love? Does she show little interest in things she used to love to do?
- Has your child shown dramatic shifts in eating or sleeping patterns? For example, he used to love to eat, but now hardly touches his food; or she's always liked to sleep moderately late, but now she never even gets out of bed.
- Does your teen show extremely low energy levels? Unhealthy levels of apathy or boredom?

These are all factors to think about when considering behavioral symptoms of depression. Keep in mind that some factors, like sleep, for example, can vary and shift with the onset of adolescence anyway, so it is key to compare levels of such behaviors with what was normal for your child already.

Eating Disorders

Other forms of internalizing disorders that have become a huge concern for our society in general, and for parents of teens in particular, involve disordered eating behaviors. To be clear, I am not referring to teens' preference for pizza, chips, and soda over fruits, vegetables, and water, as this may be unhealthy but not necessarily disordered. Nor am I focusing on the tendency for teens to seemingly eat us out of house and home with their incessant snacking and frequent visits to the pantry and fridge—with two teens in my house, my kitchen often looks like a swarm of locusts has attacked and not only eaten all the food but left the cabinets and drawers open in the process. (I'm fairly certain that I've paid the local grocery store enough of my pay to build a new wing in my name.) Finally, despite the fact that obesity is a serious problem in the United States, with obesity rates in children and teens skyrocketing to alarming rates in the past few years, I will not discuss adolescent obesity in detail. What I am writing about in this section is a narrow set of truly disordered patterns of eating behaviors that can be both physically and psychologically harmful to our teens.

Eating disorders are serious but treatable illnesses that have medical and psychiatric aspects. The most prevalent and commonly known eating disorders in the U.S. are anorexia nervosa (AN) and bulimia nervosa (BN). Some of you may be wondering, why should we be alarmed? Are eating disorders among teens *that* serious a concern? The answer is, without a doubt, yes, they are. The scary truth is that eating disorders in the U.S. have reached epidemic levels, and they impact all segments of society (similar to depression, eating disorders do not discriminate). What's worse, in addition to the fact that there is no guaranteed comprehensive

cure, eating disorders can become chronic and even life threat-
ening if not recognized and treated appropriately. And, because
of the nature of these disorders (specifically as they impact adolescents), effective treatment is extremely difficult, with many, if
not most, teens relapsing multiple times over the course of their
lifetimes. Of reported cases of eating disorders in the U.S. (many
statistics are available but these most likely represent an underestimate because of the shame and stigma associated with the illness),
86 percent note the onset of symptoms by the age of twenty (peak
age of onset is fourteen to eighteen) and 77 percent report the
duration of the illness to be from one to fifteen years. What this
means is that the number of teens tormented by eating disorders is
staggering, and that the battle to overcome these illnesses can go
on for years.

With regard to gender, women in general and young women in
particular are much more likely than men to develop an eating disorder. Only an estimated 5 to 15 percent of people with anorexia or
bulimia are male. This is not to say that men are somehow immune
to developing eating disorders, as trends indicate that the prevalence rates for men are increasing steadily. But, for many reasons,
including societal expectations, media influences, peer pressure,
and genetic predisposition, women are more prone to engaging in
unhealthy behaviors in efforts to control their weight.

Because eating disorders are becoming more prevalent in the
U.S., especially among young people, there are a few things that
we, as parents, should take time to think about. First, and most
striking, is the fact that the increasing emphasis on thinness in
our society (especially for women) is occurring at exactly the same
time that the population in the U.S. is becoming heavier, therefore setting unrealistic expectations and, again, sending our young

people mixed messages. Further, 30 to 67 percent of normal-weight adolescent and college girls believe they are overweight, and, even more shocking, 80 percent of *all* women report being dissatisfied with their bodies. And finally, 13.4 percent of young girls and 7.1 percent of young boys are engaged in disordered eating patterns, which underscores the social problem that is spinning out of control in this country. And because factors associated with disordered eating include low self-esteem, depression, substance use, and suicidal ideation, we are called upon to inform ourselves about why this is happening to our teens at such alarming rates.

Now that I have given you a basic overview of eating disorders, I will offer more specific information on the disorders that we hear about most: anorexia and bulimia. First, because this book is written for parents of teens, a brief note on the parents' perspective. Having a child with anorexia is one of the most frightening, frustrating, and exhausting experiences a parent may go through in a lifetime. In addition to the constant worry and stress involved in watching their children literally starve themselves and the suffering they feel as they watch their teens in such agony over the very concept of weight, parents of anorexics feel absolutely helpless and full of guilt. They wonder what they could have done differently. They tend to think, "Maybe if I simply tell her more often that I love her or if I talk to her more, or in a different way, or if I get her the help she needs...everything will be okay, and she will see the reality of the situation: that she is beautiful just the way she is, and that she is only harming herself in attempting to lose even more weight." But the sad truth is that, more often than not, all of these efforts seem futile, as the disease persists in its unrelenting and debilitating grip on teens, leaving parents feeling helpless, hopeless, angry, and devastated. What exactly is this disease, and how can we, as parents of teens, identify it in our own teens?

Anorexia Nervosa

Anorexia nervosa involves excessive self-induced weight loss or refusal to maintain weight at or above the minimal normal weight for a person's age and height (i.e., more than 15 percent *below* expected body weight). This means that people with anorexia become dangerously thin and are obsessed with weighing themselves and with the way others may "see" them. Onset of this disease usually occurs after puberty or in late adolescence, and it is experienced primarily by girls and young women, as it is fairly rare in males. It strikes approximately 1 percent of the female population, but again, this may well be a dramatic underestimate. Interestingly, because of the expectations and pressures associated with participation in modeling, dance, and gymnastics, anorexia has been shown to be prevalent among those who pursue these types of careers.

Anorexia nervosa is the deadliest of all psychiatric illnesses and, if left untreated or in the event of unsuccessful treatment, it can lead to heart failure, organ failure, malnutrition, or even death or suicide. People who suffer with this disease have an intense drive for thinness, and experience an irrational and even morbid fear of gaining weight. This constant fear is irrational because, despite the anorexic person's weight already being dangerously low, all she sees when she looks in the mirror is fat, a perception called body image distortion. People who suffer with this disease look in the mirror and use descriptors such as fat, ugly, stupid, unlikable, and unlovable; they tend to equate tremendously negative opinions of themselves (which go beyond looks) with their weight. What is truly difficult to comprehend is that, although anorexics can see the numbers on the scale (they weigh themselves many, many times per day) and know that they may weigh only a fraction of what they should weigh compared with others their age, they still have a desperate and uncontrollable need to lose even more weight. And so they do whatever it takes to reach these unsustainable and unhealthy goals, essentially starving themselves. To make things even more complicated and challenging, people with anorexia often experience comorbidities. That is, they may also deal with depression, anxiety, obsessive/compulsive thoughts and behaviors, and other psychological disturbances. The following list describes, in brief, some of the signs and symptoms of anorexia nervosa:

- Frequently feeling cold compared with others, due to insufficient body fat
- Hair loss/thinning scalp hair
- Development of lanugo hair (fair, downy hair on face and back)
- Decreased blood pressure/dizziness
- Decreased heart rate
- Dry skin, brittle nails
- Missed periods (females); due to insufficient body fat, reproductive system shuts down
- Sadness, depression, moodiness, irritability
- Sensitive, perfectionistic nature; self-critical features
- Decreased levels of testosterone (males)

Bulimia Nervosa

Like anorexia, bulimia nervosa involves a serious preoccupation with food, weight, and body image. People with bulimia engage in recurrent episodes of binge eating, characterized by eating abnormally large amounts of food in short periods of time, as well as a sense of losing control during the episode. Because a bulimic binge is typically followed by guilt, shame, and anxiety, what usually follows are recurrent compensatory behaviors (purging) to prevent weight gain. These behaviors can include vomiting regularly after binges or meals, taking laxatives or diuretics, or taking diet pills, or they may be less invasive practices, such as excessive exercise (in some cases, running or working out for hours) or fasting (sometimes for days). Similar to those with anorexia, people with bulimia are also overly concerned with body weight and image.

Onset of bulimia usually occurs during late adolescence or early adulthood and affects approximately 1 to 3 percent of the population. Those who suffer with bulimia are well aware that their eating patterns (binging and purging) are unhealthy and abnormal, and they feel frustrated and ashamed by that knowledge. Nonetheless, bulimia is much more prevalent than anorexia, with many undetected and unreported cases going untreated. Despite the many similarities in the disordered thinking and behavior around food, a person's weight has little to do with bulimia, whereas the criterion for an anorexia diagnosis is that a person is 15 percent or more below her expected body weight. This means that, although anorexia becomes relatively easy to identify based on the massive weight loss, bulimia can go unnoticed for a very long time, as sufferers look "normal" with respect to weight. Some of the signs and symptoms of bulimia include:

- Dehydration/electrolyte disturbances, from vomiting, laxatives, or diuretics
- Constipation
- Irregular menstruation in women
- Broken blood vessels in eyes, from vomiting often
- Sore, irritated throat
- Low energy/fatigue
- Stomach ulcers/bloating
- Abrasions of knuckles, from sticking fingers down their throats
- Irregular heartbeat, low blood pressure
- Depression, anxiety, guilt or shame, low self esteem

Time for a Change

It is time for a paradigm shift of sorts: we all need to carefully examine media portrayals of beauty and thinness, and look at how they are potentially harming our children on an all-too-regular basis. It is also time for advocates to call for specific changes to policies that allow pro-ana and pro-mia sites ("thinspiration" websites on which people with anorexia or bulimia give others tips on how to succeed in their goals of losing more weight) to continue reinforcing or encouraging our young people to engage in self-harming behaviors. We must all band together to make changes for our young people, and we must do it soon.

As with depression, we know that genetics and environment each play a role in perpetuating the problem of eating disorders in our country. As physician and researcher Dr. Walter Kaye points out in his article titled "Comorbidity of Anxiety Disorders with Anorexia and Bulimia Nervosa," "We think genes load the gun by creating behavioral susceptibility such as perfectionism or the drive for thinness. Environment then pulls the trigger."[5] In that case, parents of teens with eating disorders are left with the task of trying to figure out the best and most effective treatment plan for their child. Again, there is no silver bullet that will magically solve all problems for those with eating disorders, but we do know that there are some excellent inpatient and outpatient clinics with experts who are ready and willing to help. There are many local and national resources that have the specific mission of providing both information and solutions to individuals and their families who are struggling with these illnesses. So, if you are one of those families, know that you are not alone and that there are many, many families out there in the same difficult situation, dealing with the same challenges and struggles.

If you have been fortunate enough to have escaped the notorious impact that disordered eating has on teens and their families, you are now, at minimum, well informed and equipped to handle any future situation that may arise. In any case, I once again offer up the advice that you should talk and *listen* to your teen. Although keeping a finger on the pulse of what teens are thinking and how they are feeling is a real challenge, you can, at minimum, let them know that you are interested in what they are going through, are willing to help in any way possible, and will love and support them no matter what.

Unconditional Love & Support

If we parents were all to look back on our adolescent years, we would probably agree that being a teenager is really hard. Teens are faced with all sorts of pressures, expectations, insecurities, and doubts, and must manage them across several different contexts: family, peers, academics, social groups, romantic relationships, and so on. And in today's world, which moves at lightning speed, with peers watching and judging instantly via social networking sites, it is no wonder that teens are feeling stressed. But, remember that you, as a parent, have the unique opportunity to make a big difference in your young person's life. And contrary to the messages they send us about needing independence and *not* wanting to spend time with us, our teens need us more now than ever. We *are* the most important people, and we provide the most important influence, in our teens' lives. Of course they will continue to push limits; it's their job! But teens need to feel the safety net of our unconditional love and support, and more than anything, they need us to listen. So, go on parents, I challenge you to be informed, be brave, and be there for your teens. They *will* appreciate it eventually. I can *almost* guarantee it.

9

The Sandwich Generation

Facing the Fears and Insecurities of Being a Parent of a Teen

Being a good parent is one of the most difficult yet rewarding jobs a person can have. Being the parent of a teen, in particular, is a daunting task, especially given the fast-paced, technology-driven, competitive society we live in today. As we begin to notice the significant changes that come with adolescence (physical changes brought about by puberty, the constant angst and moodiness, and, of course, the classic eye rolling inevitably accompanied by the I-know-it-all attitude), we wonder what happened to our happy, affectionate little boy or girl. As our children get older, we are inevitably amazed to witness our sweet child mutate into a full-blown pubescent mass of emotions. We also begin to search for answers to a multitude of questions in an effort to understand what's normal and what's not during our child's transition to adulthood, see how other parents are handling this tumultuous time, and learn what resources are out there to keep us from pulling our hair out and help us figure out if we're doing *anything* right.

Lost and Bewildered

It is safe to say that thousands of parents find themselves feeling lost, unprepared, and uncertain when they are faced with raising a teenager. Just the other day, I overheard a conversation between two dads at the gym. Dad number one was expressing his disbelief and utter frustration at his teenage son's newfound snarky attitude and unwelcome behavior. He proceeded to express even more frustration and self-doubt as he explained how he had handled the situation, wondering, with considerable trepidation, if he had done the right thing. Dad number two, joined by several other dads who were also eavesdropping on the conversation, responded by exclaiming, "Oh God, I'm so happy to hear you say this...I thought I was the only one dealing with this crap, and I'm *always* wondering if I even know what I'm doing!"

Suffice it to say, parents of teens have many questions, doubts, fears, and insecurities. In fact, several recent national publications underscore the fact that there are tons of parents out there thirsty for information on parenting teenagers. *The New York Times*, for example, recently published a piece highlighting a growing demand by readers for "...more on parenting teens, please!" To which the *Times* responded by pointing out that *Brain, Child* magazine, a widely distributed and wildly popular source, had devoted an entire issue to the topic. Bottom line: we are all wondering if we're doing this whole parenting teens thing right. After all, physically creating a person was easy, but raising them to be kind, responsible, informed, non-ax-murderers is the hard part. That's a lot of pressure! And with adolescents reportedly making up one quarter of the world's population, it is no wonder that there are so many parents out there in a total state of panic. I hear you.

So, where can we turn for answers or advice? The answer most of us think of immediately is the Internet. But finding reliable answers on the Internet can be overwhelming when you consider that entering the words "parenting teens" in one popular search engine brings up more than 91,700,000 results in .44 seconds. What's more, you've got to sift through the millions of sites to determine which ones are relevant, which are legitimate, and which contain reliable, valid, and useful information. Who has the time?

What happened to the good old-fashioned method of talking and bouncing ideas off other parents? When our children were really young, we had a virtual army of parents to lean on, get advice from, and maybe even just vent to. Back then, we would attend playgroups and interact with other moms and dads on the playground, and we had no problem sharing our cute stories and seeking advice on the latest and greatest parenting techniques, preschools, or diaper ointment. But as our children become teens, we not only lose time with them, we also lose our built-in playground support group and resource guides. Bummer. This is the very reason I'm writing this book, for parents just like me, who wonder on a daily basis, "Am I doing anything right?" when it comes to raising my teens.

In this chapter, I'll provide insight into what most parents at this stage in life go through, to let you know that you are not alone. If, at any point in time during your child's teen years, you have questions or wonder if it's normal to think or feel a certain way, chances are there are thousands of parents out there thinking, wondering, and feeling just as you do. So, let's imagine that we're sitting together, as a newly formed circle of friends, having coffee (or margaritas!) and sharing information, shall we?

Our Own Perspective

Unless you had your child at the age of six, you are probably in the "middle-aged adult" category—for our teens, of course, this means that we're essentially older than dirt. Regardless, this period in our lives presents us with many unique challenges and stressors, and adjusting to our kids' journey through adolescence may take more of a toll on our mental health than it does on theirs. Go figure, right? I should note, however, that not all parents experience these issues in the same way or to the same extent. For example, parents who are extremely involved in gratifying work outside the home, or who have an especially happy and supportive marriage or partnership, may be buffered against some of these negative consequences, whereas single mothers may be especially vulnerable to the effects of living with a moody teen. They may even be driven to write a book on the subject! Variations notwithstanding, following are some of the struggles that parents of teens share.

A couple of years ago, my family took a trip to the lake. Once there, my daughter Sophia walked out wearing a bright purple, eye-catching, and very small bikini, and grabbed just about everyone's attention. Because, compared with the previous summer, she filled out the suit quite nicely, my friend, who was there with her kids, exclaimed, "Holy crap, Sara, you're in trouble!" This outburst was followed closely by, "God, I remember when I looked like that!"

Some parents, upon seeing their teenage son or daughter develop into a mature, attractive, and even sexy person, begin to feel increased concern about *their own* bodies, physical attractiveness, and sexual appeal. This is especially true of single parents, who, both because of the pressures that come with the youth-focused society in which we live and because they may consider themselves still "on the market" and possibly in search of new companionship, feel a certain level of pressure to remain vigilant about such things as physical appearance and attractiveness. As we see our children reach the pinnacle of physical beauty (at least as it is defined by many in our society), we begin to lament the undeniable fact that we are no longer in our teens or twenties, and, despite our efforts, time, gravity, and loss of epidermal elasticity begin to take their toll on us physically. We begin to wonder, "Am I attractive anymore?" and "Will anyone find me sexually appealing?" As you can imagine, all this self-doubt and insecurity tends to do quite a number on our self-esteem and self-confidence. If you've never felt this way, and are wondering who in their right mind would entertain such vain or inappropriate thoughts, just know that there are many (and I mean *many*) parents who have, and to them I say, you are not alone. It's totally normal to feel this way, and guess what? It's okay.

Something else that parents of teens tend to experience is what is called the *occupational plateau*. That is, around middle age, we may come to the realization that perhaps we have gone as far or climbed as high as we can in our careers. You've heard of the glass ceiling that women and minorities reportedly reach, right? Well, this is the "getting old" version, whereby we either reach our goals at work and really have no where else to go, we get bored and are no longer interested in doing the same thing year after year, or we're replaced by young, fresh people, straight out of college who have young, fresh ideas and methods. In any case, we may feel outdated, frustrated, and stuck, and may begin to question our career effectiveness and choices. Along those same lines, people at this stage of life also begin to recognize that, unlike when we were young and vibrant and could reinvent ourselves on a whim, the possibilities are no longer endless; rather, the opportunities for change are limited, and seem to be getting more so as each day passes. I know that this may sound rather hyperbolic, as droves of people *do* start new careers, begin to travel, or choose to take new and exciting paths once their children are older, but many people feel at an impasse during this transitional stage of their lives, and for those people, I repeat, you are not alone.

Hoagies

Now, for a discussion of the "sandwich generation." The *what* generation? Perhaps you had not realized, until now, that a name exists for our particular cohort; sadly, it is not one of those cool group references like "generation X, Y, or Z" or "the millennials." No, my friends, our group—whose membership is defined by the need to care for aging parents while also supporting children (teens)—is likened to a cold piece of deli meat stuck between two slices of bread. Nice. The point is that, for many of us, we are indeed caught between caring for our elderly parents (not easy) and raising our teens (definitely not easy), which leaves us feeling tired, anxious, and stressed about finances, our personal time (or lack thereof), health, and career development.

Throughout this book, we've discussed the various challenges that we, as parents, face when raising teenagers. At no point in time did anyone warn me that, in addition to the rollercoaster ride of emotions and responsibilities that go along with raising teens, I would simultaneously face the fact that my parents are getting older and may quite possibly need my help. This unexpected role reversal is unsettling at best. Don't get me wrong, I am by no means complaining, as I feel honored to be able to give back to the two people who not only gave me life, but who have always been there for me, my brothers, and all thirteen of their grandchildren. There is absolutely nothing my parents wouldn't do for any of us, and now it's our turn to care for them. I simply had no idea it would be this hard.

Those of us in this situation (the challenges loom so large, perhaps I should rename us the "hoagie generation") know that this situation is painfully difficult for two reasons. First, it is simply heart wrenching to watch your parents, whom you are so used to seeing as strong, active, and energetic, slow down and physically deteriorate right before your eyes.

As a developmentalist, I am fully aware of the gradual decline that we all inevitably experience. But as a daughter, I watch the two people who fought off monsters when I was a little girl; who stood strong and defended me against the mean girls in junior high; who took care of me all night when I was sick; who had the boundless energy to run us all to various practices, games, performances, and *still* suggest that we go outside and throw the ball around; and I realize that when it comes to your own parents, it's just different. Witnessing your parents' decline is not only humbling, it also feels like reality just walked up to you and slapped you across the face. It makes you realize that we're all here for only a short while and then we're not. To be sure, seeing my parents get older, and being ready to take care of *them* when *they're* sick, has definitely made me more aware of my own mortality, but it has also made me appreciate every second of every day.

Here's the second reason the sandwich generation is in such a tough predicament: let's say you've dealt with the reality that your parents are not as sprightly as they used to be and may have health problems, need help getting to appointments, and so on, but guess what? The other three thousand items on your daily to-do list—everything from feeding dogs to buying groceries to paying bills to meeting work deadlines to doing laundry to, lest we forget, helping your teens and *their* long list of to-dos—are all still there. Every day. I'm exhausted just thinking about it all. It's not just tiring, it's downright stressful. All too often, parents of teens feel overwhelmed because they are pulled in so many different directions. It's nice to be needed, but sometimes it seems just a bit ridiculous, don't you think? Especially as your aging parents begin to experience declines in their health, taking care of them while also caring for your own children is not only time consuming, it can also have negative impacts on sleep, relaxation, and self-care, and can even lead to tremendous stress, burnout, and depression.

Giving Yourself a Little TLC

So, what is a "hoagie" to do? Before considering this, I suggest that you go and pour yourself a nice cup of tea, glass of wine, or whatever it is that signals to you it is time to relax and be good to yourself. I would now like to invite you to forego the notion of selfishness for a moment. Just for a few minutes, let's suspend the strongly held parental belief that if we think or do *anything* for ourselves, we are, by definition, being selfish...or worse yet, bad parents. I am often asked, "How in the world do you do it all?" and my answer is almost always a resounding, "I really don't know, I just do!" But the truth is that I *do* know. I know that in reality, I never have to bear the heavy weight of responsibility alone. I have friends, family, and even online resources to help me distribute the load and manage the weight. I'm no martyr, nor do I try to be. I recognize that there are times when I feel as though I'm drowning, and at those times I reach out to those who will help pull me to safety. My parents, my brothers, and my friends (all of whom have kids, and therefore also experience the deep and dangerous waters of parental obligations) have saved my sanity on many occasions; and I've been there to save theirs as well. We are there for one another, and it admittedly feels pretty good. Some might say, what if your family is not close, or what if you don't have family in town at all? To this I say that family doesn't necessarily mean people to whom you are biologically linked. Although I know it might be difficult to admit that you need a little help, there are so many resources out there for parents just like us: friends, online groups, community organizations, neighbors, parenting bloggers, etc. The help is there, all we have to do is ask for it.

I also know very well that I have to be good to myself. I have to take care of myself, if I am to be around (and maintain the ability) to care for others. There are plenty of times when I think to myself: If I'm always the one taking care of everyone else, who will take care of me? I call these my very own personal "pity parties," and rarely is anyone but me invited. I've even told friends that I liken my situation, as a single mother of teens who happens to have older parents, to a house of cards. At the very bottom of this staggeringly tall house of cards is a single card that provides the foundation (I am the metaphorical lone card, if you hadn't guessed!). This base card is strong, and it carries the entire load of the house above it. But if anything were to happen to this bedrock card, well, the entire house would collapse and come crashing down. And *this*, my friends, would not be good. I mean, really, who has time to get sick? (This, of course, is a bit of a hyperbole, as you may recall me mentioning the fact that I have one of the most fantastic support systems in the world—my parents.)

My point in sharing with you my house of cards story is that parents of teens who also worry about and/or care for their aging parents, *and* who have the responsibilities of job, house, car, etc., often feel as though the weight of the world sits squarely on their shoulders. You may be familiar with this feeling. But the reality is that, in order to effectively sustain and maintain all that the house of cards represents, we must be sure to take care of ourselves. I am referring here to eating right, exercising, getting enough sleep, and doing all the things we can to care for ourselves physically. But more than that, I'm talking about giving ourselves a break, practicing a bit of self-compassion, and maybe even recognizing that we just may be modern-day superheroes!

I read a great piece on the *Huffington Post* recently titled "This Is How to Win at Parenting and Life" that really hit home for me.[1] The author invited us to challenge that voice in our heads that's always telling us that we're not good enough—at being a partner, mother, father, friend, or worker. The author suggested that we retrain that voice today so that, instead of constantly beating ourselves up about the things we *haven't* accomplished or *didn't* do exactly right or on time, we focus on the positive things we *have* accomplished. I know I am my own harshest critic—if self-deprecating thinking were illegal, I would be guilty beyond a shadow of a doubt, and be sentenced to the worst sort of punishment (feeling badly about myself!). For this, I offer myself a sincere and heartfelt mea culpa. None of us is perfect, and we will *all*, at one point or another, lose our cool with our teens, miss a deadline by a little (or a lot), forget to pick up dog food (again), or simply be too damn tired to cook dinner—and you know what? It is totally okay.

Like our teens, we are works in progress. Masterpieces, in fact. It really *is* time for us to retrain that voice in our heads to appreciate, respect, and even congratulate ourselves for the amazing things we do every day. And what is considered *amazing*? Everything. Not just the major accomplishments or formal recognitions, but the small victories, too: the fact that we take another breath and the next step so that our family has us to lean on; the fact that we have not only given life, but are making it better for the people we care for most by being present; the fact that, in the face of deadlines, pressures, and immense responsibilities, we can smile and actually appreciate the chaotic bliss that is life. At the risk of sounding horribly clichéd, life is too short to spend feeling bad about ourselves. We are on this planet for a blink, and then it's over, so why not savor and appreciate everything: the good and the bad, the big and the small. And why not give ourselves a break while we're at it? Though we may feel small at times, we are fierce warriors who, every once in a while, need a little kindness and compassion; and who better to give it to us than the person we know best... ourselves. So the next time you start mentally beating yourself up for something you *didn't* do, remember this: you are doing everything right. Even the most monumental of screwups is brilliant, because you are in the arena, committed to doing your very best, and you never, ever give up. As Teddy Roosevelt once said in his speech "Citizenship in a Republic":

> It is not the critic who counts; not the [wo]man who points out how the strong [wo]man stumbles, or where the doer of deeds could have done them better. The credit belongs to the [wo]man who is actually in the arena, whose face is marred by dust and sweat and blood; who strives valiantly; who errs, who comes short again and again, because there is no effort without error and shortcoming; but who does

actually strive to do the deeds; who knows great enthusiasms, the great devotions; who spends himself in a worthy cause; who at the best knows in the end the triumph of high achievement, and who at the worst, if he fails, at least fails while daring greatly, so that his place shall never be with those cold and timid souls who neither know victory nor defeat.[2]

So, be good to yourself, because you, my friend, deserve it.

10

On Letting Go

Embracing the Transition as Your Teen Moves Out

I have decidedly become a sentimental old fool. I didn't used to be this way, and I totally blame my kids for it. Here is why I have suddenly become a big pile of emotional mush: my kids are growing up, moving out, living their own lives, and there is absolutely nothing I can do about it. What was that John Mayer song about not being able to stop the train, meaning time or life or something like that? I love/hate that song. It's not that I'm lonely or afraid; I have many good friends, a healthy social life, and more work than I can possibly handle. I'd say, as a career-oriented individual, I'm pretty happy and satisfied with the trajectory my life has taken. Here is where the "but" comes in. As a mother, I'm a hot mess. There are times when my heart actually aches for my children. I miss them, and I worry about them...and, get this, they all live within a few miles of me, so it's not like I go months without seeing them. Crazy? Melodramatic? Maybe. I have never been one of those stereotypical, overreacting moms whose entire life is defined by and lived for her children—but now that they're not around every day to cook for, clean up after, talk to, or even argue with, my world is undergoing a seismic shift, and I'm not sure I like it. Like I said … a hot mess.

When our children get to the point of moving on because they are going off to college, getting a job, or just moving out, we are randomly and unexpectedly hit by a massive wave of nostalgia. To be clear, this is not the scene that some may imagine: parents sitting in their perpetually clean, quiet, and organized home with a glass of wine in hand, reminiscing about the good times we had when the kids were little … although this does happen every now and then. The wave I'm talking about feels strangely like a huge, gaping hole in your chest that can either drop you to your knees or make you sick to your stomach, or both. What is this? Why am I feeling this way after I have essentially accomplished what I've worked so hard all my adult life to achieve: successfully raising my children to be strong, independent, and productive human beings in their own right? The answer is that—although your children are strong and independent, and look, to 99.9 percent of the people they meet, like fully mature adults—what *you* see when you look at them is the rosy-cheeked little boy whose favorite pastime was twirling your hair in his fingers while you read him a bedtime story or the wide-eyed little girl who used to ride on your shoulders and giggle at every one of your lame jokes. When you look at your grown-up child, what you see is your baby, who now happens to reside in a big person's body instead of a little person's—but still your baby.

Everything and everyone else around us may have successfully made the transition with time, recognizing our children as fully capable young adults, but once these pangs of nostalgia come over us, it's like logic and reason go out the window and our emotions take over and run the show. If any of this rings a bell for you, know that you are in the company of many other emotionally disheveled parents, and we can share a tissue box together sometime. If, on the other hand, your kiddo is still too young for you to even consider this a realistic scenario, or if you find yourself so deep in adolescent angst that you can't wait for the day your teen is off on her own, then just hang on and wait. The day will come when you think, "Ah . . . so *this* is what she was blubbering about."

When our children are in the throes of adolescence, with all its trials and tribulations, what we fail to recognize (because we can't see the trees through the proverbial angst-ridden teen forest) is that time goes by so unbelievably fast; before we know it, they are grown and gone. What's more, the very shape of our daily lives changes completely once they're gone. We tend to take the little things for granted when we're in the thick of it all, but as soon as the teen tornado has passed, we miss all the action. When our kids were living at home, they were, whether we realized it or not, central to our daily routine. Think about it. This is what my daily routine looks like, for just a few more precious months, until my second teen goes off to college:

7:00 a.m.	Wake teen for school (round one, no success)
7:15	Wake teen for school (round two, see stirring and hear grumbling)
7:30	Wake teen (round three, and she will now have to step up her pace, which means I officially become the morning nag)
7:45	Greet the walking dead with a cheerful "Good morning, sweetie," get more grumbles in return

8:00   Head out for work, give teen one last push out the door, as she will now officially be late, but her hair is not completely straight; tragic

8:30   Finally leave the house; we're both late

9:00   Work all day, but intercept several texts throughout the day from teen with questions like: "Can you pick up a black binder on your way home? My project is due tomorrow morning, can you help?"; "What's for dinner? I'm starving and you didn't give me any lunch money!"; "I'm going to my friend's after school, is that ok? She's gonna help me with homework"; "Can we go buy those boots that I really wanted after school?" And my recent favorite, "We have a big potluck thing planned today in sixth-period Spanish class, can you bring me some of your homemade enchiladas?"

4:45 p.m.   Think about what to make for dinner, with one teen insisting on eating superhealthy (and only organic, of course) and the other (home from college only to eat my free food) wanting sloppy joes

5:00   Leave work and go to grocery store (because text from teens explicitly stated that "We never have any food in the house," even though the local grocer could build a new wing at the store in my name because I shop there *every day* and spend gobs of money)

6:30   Make dinner while teens compare notes on school (high school versus college), the lame teachers, and hot girls and boys in college; I enjoy the witty, teen version of repartee

7:30	Try to have a sit-down family dinner with teens; fairly successful, though I have to guilt them a couple of times (notice I did not say lecture them because that would be nagging) about not texting fifteen other people while real people sit right in front of them at the dinner table
8:15	Say loving goodbye to college teen, ask home teen to help clean kitchen; listen to full-blown, Supreme Court–level argument presented by home teen over why college teen *never* has to help clean or do *anything*, because he is *obviously* my favorite... oh, the injustice of it all (my teen daughter should seriously consider becoming an attorney)
8:20	Clean kitchen alone, in peace
8:30	Ask teen about homework, to which she responds, "Ugh, Mom, I'm just trying to relax for a minute... it's been a long day, and I'm tired."
9:00	Ask teen about homework again (more like *told* teen to do homework), and now officially become the evening nag
9:30	Teen snugly locked away in her room, with TV on, music on, phone exploding, doing homework; time to catch my breath, relax, and have some down time (right)
9:40	Log on to computer to prepare lectures for next day's class; also, make dental appointment for teen, help with homework, review/edit college essays and applications, and complete FAFSA
11:00	Completely exhausted and on the way to bed; but wait, teen is up, finished with homework, and

	wide awake, texting, chatting, talking, Instagramming, Facebooking, tweeting with friends; tell her to go to bed
11:30	Teen still awake, and seemingly rejuvenated; I am delirious; I insist teen turn off electronics and go to bed (again), officially becoming late-night nag
12 a.m.	Finally in bed, enjoying the quiet and stillness, thinking about the one thousand things to be done tomorrow; teen comes in and kisses me goodnight

Notice that almost every thought, action, or emotion somehow involves my dependent children. And guess what? Tomorrow I get to wake up and do it all over again. Isn't that wonderful? I know some of you may read this and conclude that I am 100 percent insane—a complete lunatic, in fact. And perhaps you're right. But, despite the frenzied madness and feverish pace, this whirlwind of a daily life suits me just fine. I have become quite accustomed to it. It's chaotic bliss, and I love it, because it makes me feel needed. It gives me a strange sense of parental satisfaction. I am doing what I consider to be *the* most basic and most *important* job I can do: providing for my children. But, what is going to happen to me once my home teen turns into my second college teen? What will my daily routine look like then? Will I shrivel up in my useless maternal state, all alone, except for the hundred cats I will live with, so as to have *someone* to take care of? Not likely (oh yeah, I still have my eight-year-old), but as my third child prepares to head off in search of her new and exciting life in college, it certainly feels like this could be my plight.

Permission to Grieve

I know many parents out there wonder if they are the only ones feeling upset as their children grow up and move out. For a long time, I was actually a bit embarrassed to confess my parental sorrows to people. It felt a little silly or petty compared to, say, someone losing a son or daughter to cancer or some other illness. I was afraid that perhaps my perspectives and feelings were somehow a consequence of inappropriate attachments or some sort of unhealthy codependent relationship I had fostered—yes, I *am* a psychologist working overtime.

The more I talked to parents with older teens going off to college, however, the more I realized that feelings of loss are a fairly common experience. What a relief! In fact, what I realize now is that some parents not only acknowledge the normality of it all, they go a step further and suggest that we parents of older teens give ourselves permission to grieve when our children move out. This perspective not only piqued my interest, it made me feel reassured that (1) I'm not losing my mind and (2) others have gone through it and made it to the other side just fine.

The brilliance of this viewpoint lies in the two key words: *permission* and *grief*. First, I love the idea of giving ourselves permission because it is so simple and so obvious, yet we, as parents of teens, rarely do it. From the very first time we held that new baby in our arms, we have had to be responsible, dedicated, and selfless. Our children come first, and that's it. There was no rulebook or manual to tell us this, we just knew that being a good parent required that we put our child's needs before our own. Because of this, it always felt counterintuitive and, well, just wrong to put ourselves first. But the concept of permission allows us to free ourselves from this unspoken obligation (if just for a while, as we know our children will always maintain their priority status) and accept what we are feeling, focusing for a while on what *we* need.

Second, the concept of grief centers around loss. This does not have to mean loss of a loved one to a fatality, it can mean simply not having someone in your life in the same way anymore. When our grown children move out, we come to realize that this is the end of the relationship we had, yet it is also the beginning of a new and very different relationship. Our children are becoming truly independent, and the daily connection you had, where you not only saw your kid every day but delighted in her dependence and thrived on the chaos, is now gone. The relationship has taken a major turn, and now you may see your child rarely and you are no longer needed in the same way. This relational shift, although we knew it was coming and spent years anticipating it, feels sudden and unwelcome. We really do experience a loss, and it hurts. The point is that it is okay to acknowledge and embrace these feelings; we should give ourselves permission to experience the loss and learn from the experience, so we can move forward with a stronger sense of self-compassion and appreciation of the new and improved, more grown-up relationship with our child.

A Note on Boomerang Kids

To put into perspective our feelings of loss at our kids moving out, we should also consider that some parents find themselves in completely different circumstances. Some older adolescents move out, experience life for a bit, decide for one reason or another that it is too difficult, then move back in—and don't ever leave. Some have termed this cohort of grown children "boomerang kids." Clever. An article in the *New York Times* titled "It's Official: The Boomerang Kids Won't Leave" recently noted that one in five people in their twenties and thirties have moved back home to live with parents.

Economic trends are cited as the main culprit for this phenomenon, but regardless of the reason, the outcome makes me wonder how *those* parents feel. I'm quite certain that some of these parents experience the opposite of my empty nest version of teens leaving the home, and feel happy and content to have their "child" still snuggled in the bosom of his childhood home. Conversely, I'm sure that some parents of "boomerangers" hope that maybe, just maybe, one day, before they die, they will have the house to themselves and be free of parental responsibilities. I bet it's a little bit of both. Either way, the relationship between parents and their grown children changes: teens feel liberated and parents are left feeling confused and perhaps bit lost, faced with what seems like sudden and jolting alterations within the family. There is no right or wrong way to handle these seismic shifts in the relationship with your older child, as it is a matter of what works for you and your family, but the shifts occur regardless. And, it's okay. We should accept these as familial growing pains. Our child is getting older and moving on (in whatever form that takes), and therefore, our family dynamics also change and grow. Growth and development...that's what life's all about, isn't it?

Interestingly, there are cultural differences when it comes to the expectation of a grown child moving out. I come from a very large, very traditional Mexican, Catholic family, and with this group of people, as in many other Latino households, it is *not* assumed that the child will move out as soon as he finishes high school. Quite the contrary (my mother cried when I had the audacity to move out to go to college). In fact, the assumption is that (grown) children will stay at home as long as humanly possible—or until they get married—and even then, it is quite possible that the entire clan will cohabitate in one very large, very loud and loving abode. But whether you expect it or not, whether it is sudden or gradual, whether your child returns home or stays away, your relationship with your older adolescent will go through a variety of transformations. See previous note on growth and development—it's all good.

Let's look on the bright side: once our teens move out, or simply move on, we now have more time to invest in other things such as, oh, I don't know... ourselves. *Gasp.* Remember when you were in the thick of it all, hair on fire with the to-do list that would never end, wishing that you had *more time*? More time to catch your breath and relax, to read a book, to start a new hobby, or just spend time catching up with friends. Well, guess what? Now, you have that time. So, make the most of it, and enjoy!

New Concerns

One thing that all parents of grown children experience is the constant worry, which we assumed would lessen as our children grew older. Boy, were we wrong. As our teens get older, and especially once they leave the house, an entirely new set of worries comes into play. Of course we still worry for their safety and wellness, as we had in the past (though now we can't expect them to call us every time they get home), but in addition we now worry about how they are adjusting (to college life, dorm or apartment living, etc.), how they are dealing with the typical struggles of life (responsibilities, deadlines, money, mean people), whether they are sad or lonely (total projection), and whether they are making any solid, lifelong friends.

My son Thomas is in his second year of college at a first-rate university just up the road, in a nearby city. It is a small, private institution, with an excellent academic reputation and top-notch security and safety standards. My son is a strong, fit young man with his mother's intellectual ability and a future so bright I can hardly contain myself when I think about it. Even so, I worry. I wonder if he's taking care of himself. I agonize over whether he will be able to handle the pressures of school, work, deadlines, girlfriends, etc. Why? *Why* do I continue to worry, even though I know he's a fully capable, grown man (sort of) attending a great school? I worry because, regardless of how old he is, how smart he is, or where he is, I am *still* his mother, he is *still* my baby, and that will never change. Just because our children get older and move on with their lives, we do not stop being their parents. Our thoughts and emotions certainly will never shift to the point of not caring what our kids do or how they are—the key is in how we manage our thoughts and feelings. If we, as parents, allowed ourselves to focus too much on the worries and what ifs, we would be buried by them, and what good would that do for anyone?

So, what *can* we do to ease the worry? Constantly check up on our grown kids by stalking them via social networking sites, phone, and text? Employ someone to "keep an eye on them" for us? This is probably not the best approach. Despite our nearly overwhelming urge to take action and do whatever it takes to ensure our grown child's well being and success, it is likely not in our (or our child's) best interest to become what some social scientists refer to as "helicopter parents." This term refers to parents who go to unreasonable lengths to help or protect their children. Typically witnessed in either academic or professional settings, helicopter parents of grown children do things like call a child's professor to ask for extensions on homework deadlines (yes, I have received these types of phone calls from parents myself), write papers or do other assignments *for* their child, or call their child's boss to ask that he get a raise. Sound extreme? That's because, to most people, it is.

Rather than doing for our children the things that they themselves should be responsible for, a better strategy is to give them the tools (i.e., instruction, tutoring, support, appropriate expectation, etc.) to accomplish these goals for themselves, and learn to let go. I know it's scary…believe me, I know. But if we were to do everything *for* them, how or when will they learn to stand on their own two feet? How will they learn about responsibility, time management, organization, scheduling, and success and failure? They are our "grown" children, after all, and much like when they were little, they will learn that after they fall and scrape their knees, they have to get right back up and keep going. Contrary to what we may think, when we protect them from natural consequences (i.e., getting an F on a paper because they didn't complete the work or getting fired from a job because they were consistently late), we are, simply put, doing our children a disservice and hindering their ability to become responsible, successful adults.

What we *can* do to help ease our concerns is communicate. Communicating with your child, as often as is comfortable for you both, via phone calls, text, or whatever means works most efficiently for you and your family, allows you to check in on how he is doing (or simply to hear his voice). Talking with other parents and friends is also helpful, to gain perspective, share stories, and maybe even vent (or sulk) a little. And finally, communicating with ourselves (internally, of course) is essential; give yourself permission to miss this kid who has played such a huge role in your life so far, and will continue to consume your heart and soul for the rest of your life, no matter how old he gets.

I would like to end this chapter by reflecting on the notion of letting go. Being a parent is likely the hardest thing you've ever had to do. I grew up in difficult circumstances, have overcome all kinds of hurdles, and earned multiple degrees as a single parent—and I can attest to the fact that parenting my children has been the most difficult, and by far, the most highly prized and valued accomplishment in my life. As parents, we invest every ounce of love, money, time, and energy into creating a person who is kind, wise, and can stand on her own two feet. And although our job is never really done, our babies *do* grow up and move on. This is the very essence of life. Yes, it is a bittersweet moment, and somewhat difficult to accept. But above and beyond anything else, what we should feel is an immense sense of pride. Pride in our children for the amazing people they are becoming; and even more, pride in ourselves for making them that way. So kudos to you, my friend. For you have not only created life, you have quite literally touched the future and made this world a better place.

CONCLUSION

Writing this book has done many things for me. It has allowed me to explore the more informal type of writing I have always wanted to do, but had never gotten the opportunity to pursue. I was trained as a researcher and academic to publish scientific work in peer-reviewed journals, so I have found it truly liberating to write in a more casual style that I find comfortable and effective. And because I see things from a parent's perspective, as well as that of an academician, it has also felt like a golden opportunity to speak directly to other parents. In the scholarly world, we typically read journals written *by* academics, *for* academics, and I've often wondered if, and when, the important information that we, as developmental psychologists, disseminate in our research findings makes its way into the homes and daily lives of the people who need it most: parents.

My goal has always been to write in a way that feels conversational and relatable, while also being accurate and informative. When I began this journey, people would ask, "What type of parenting book are you writing, a textbook?" My response, after the initial, "God, no!" was that I pictured a big group of us, all parents of teens, sitting around a very large table, sharing laughs, stories, and margaritas, while also learning from one another and feeling supported and definitely *not* alone in our experience of parenting teens. This was my intention, and I truly hope that it has come across to you in that way. I absolutely love being a mom, and especially a mom of teens. It has not only been the single most important accomplishment of my life, but it's also been the greatest honor and blessing I've ever received. Being a parent of teens is an exciting journey, and as you have likely noted, my own teens have provided me with troves of material and anecdotal evidence to support the ideas in this book, and I thank them. Without them, this book would likely not even exist.

Moving forward, I hope to write similar books that focus on single parenthood, divorce, and the chaotic world of blended families, and perhaps one that delves into my own zany Mexican family (think of the movie *My Big Fat Greek Wedding*, except we're not Greek!). These topics, as you may have gleaned, are near to my heart, and I would love to reach out and have another roundtable conversation with parents out there who have experienced similar struggles, to consider and discuss the perilous joys involved in those life experiences.

I am all too aware of how difficult times are for parents and families today. We are all rushed, stressed, burdened, and tired. Having teens, some would say, increases the stress exponentially; but I say, we should alter our perspectives and think of raising our teens not as a burden, but as a gift. As parents of teens, we get to take part in, and perhaps even influence, the beautiful transformation our children go through. It is our unfailing love and persistent commitment that helps to make them the amazing people that they become. Yes, it's a long and arduous journey. No doubt. But we mustn't forget that we are not alone. There are so many of us out there who are thinking, feeling, and wondering the same things we are. And, above all, I encourage you to savor the moments with your teens.

We've all heard the cliché about time passing in the blink of an eye, but I have to tell you, my friends, it is really true. Throughout this project, I have had to do some serious reflection, and as a consequence, have had more than a few cathartic sobbing spells. I've never been one to harbor regrets, but if there were one thing that I could do over again, it would be to spend more time with my children as they were growing up. Now that they are getting older and moving on with their own lives, I know that I will look back fondly and miss the good old days when they questioned my authority, argued every point to death, and kept me up at night worrying. Parenting teens has been a rollercoaster ride of emotions, both exhilarating and horrifying, but I have thoroughly enjoyed the ride, and I can't wait until my kids embark on the same thrilling ride with their own kids. Namaste.

NOTES

Chapter 2

1. Claudia Wallis, "What Makes Teens Tick?," *Time* magazine, May 10, 2004, 56–65.

Chapter 4

1. Laurence Steinberg, *Adolescence*, 10th edition (New York: McGraw Hill, 2014), 288.

Chapter 6

1. Catherine L. Bagwell and Michelle E. Schmidt, *Friendships in Childhood and Adolescence*, (New York: Guilford Press, 2013), 116.
2. Linda Jackson, "Adolescents and the Internet," in *The Changing Portrayal of Adolescents in the Media since 1950,* ed. Patrick Jamieson and Daniel Romer (New York: Oxford University Press, 2008), 377. David Smahel, Bradford Brown, and Lucas Blinka, "Associations Between Online Friendship and Internet Addiction Among Adolescents and Emerging Adults," *Developmental Psychology,* 48 (2012): 381–388.

Chapter 7

1. John Gottman and Nan Silver, *Why Marriages Succeed or Fail* (New York: Simon & Schuster,1994), 68.

2. Harry S. Sullivan, *The Interpersonal Theory of Psychiatry* (New York: Norton, 1953), 217.

3. Laurence Steinberg, *Adolescence*, 10th edition (New York: McGraw Hill, 2014), 336.

4. Steinberg, *Adolescence*, 336.

5. W. Andrew Collins, "More Than a Myth: The Developmental Significance of Romantic Relationships During Adolescence." *Journal of Research on Adolescence* 13 (2003): 1-24. Steinberg, *Adolescence*, 336.

6. Steinberg, *Adolescence*, 338.

Chapter 8

1. Laurence Steinberg, *Adolescence*, 10th edition (New York: McGraw Hill, 2014), 416.

2. Meich, Richard A. et.al, *Monitoring the Future: National Survey Results on Drug Use 1975–2014*, The University of Michigan Institute for Social Research: Vol 1. 2014.

3. Steinberg, *Adolescence*, 442.

4. U.S. Census Bureau, Center for Disease Control and Prevention, July 9, 2014. http://www.cdc.gov/mentalhealth/data_stats/depression-chart-txt.htm

5. Walter H. Kaye, Cynthia M. Bulik, Laura Thornton, Nicole Barbarich, and Kim Masters. "Comorbidity of Anxiety Disorders with Anorexia and Bulimia Nervosa." *American Journal of Psychiatry* 161(12) (Dec 2004): 2215–21.

Chapter 9

1. Glennon Melton, "This Is How to Win at Parenting and Life," *Huffington Post*, January 16, 2015, http://www.huffingtonpost.com/glennon-melton/this-is-how-to-win-at-parenting-and-life_b_6489048.html.

REFERENCES

Bagwell, L. and Michelle E. Schmidt. *Friendships in Childhood and Adolescence.* New York: Guilford Press, 2013.

Baumrind, Diana. "Parental Disciplinary Patterns and Social Competence in Children." *Youth and Society 9* (1978): 239–276.

Brown, Bradford. "Peer Groups." In *At the Threshold: The Developing Adolescent,* edited by S. Feldman and G. Elliott, 171–196. Cambridge, MA: Harvard University Press, 1990.

Brown, Bradford. "Adolescents' Relationships with Peers." In *Handbook of Adolescent Psychology.* edited by R. Lerner and L. Steinberg. New York: Wiley, 2004.

Carskadon. Mary. "Sleep in Adolescents: The Perfect Storm." *Pediatric Clinics of North America 58* (2011): 637–647.

Chandler, Michael. "The Othello Effect: Essay on the Emergence and Eclipse of Skeptical Doubt." *Human Development 30* (1987): 137–159.

Coleman, James. *The Adolescent Society.* Glencoe, IL: Free Press, 1961.

Fischhoff, Baruch, and Marilyn J. Quadrel,."Adolescent Alcohol Decision." In *Alcohol Problems Among Adolescents: Current Directions in Prevention Research,* edited by Gayle Boyd, John Howard, and Robert Zucker (59–84). Hillsdale, NJ: Erlbaum, 1995.

Goossens, Laurence., Inge. Seiffge-Krenke, and Alfons. Marcoen. "The Many Faces of Adolescent Egocentrism: Two European Replications." Paper presented at the biennial meetings of the Society for Research on Adolescence, Washington, DC, March 19, 1992.

Gottman, John, and Nan Silver. *What Makes Love Last? How to Build Trust and Avoid Betrayal.* New York: Simon & Schuster, 2013.

Graber, Julia, Jeannie Brooks-Gunn, Roberta Paikoff, and Michelle Warren. "Prediction of Eating Problems: An 8-Year Study of Adolescent Girls." *Developmental Psychology 30* (1994): 823–834.

Graber, Julia A., and Lisa M. Sontag. "Internalizing Problems During Adolescence." In *Handbook of Adolescent Psychology*, 3rd edition, edited by Richard Lerner & Laurence Steinberg. New York: Wiley, 2009.

Hall, Gordon S. *Adolescence.* New York: Appleton, 1904.

Jackson, Linda. "Adolescents and the Internet." In *The Changing Portrayal of Adolescents in the Media since 1950,* edited by Patrick Jamieson and Daniel Romer, 377–411. New York: Oxford University Press, 2008.

Kaiser Family Foundation Study. *Generation M2: Media in the Lives of 8- to 18-Year-Olds.* January 20, 2010.

Kaye, Walter H., Cynthia M. Bulik, Laura Thornton, Nicole Barbarich, and Kim Masters. "Comorbidity of Anxiety Disorders with Anorexia and Bulimia Nervosa." *American Journal of Psychiatry* 161(12) (Dec 2004): 2215–21.

Keating, Daniel. "Cognitive and Brain Development." In *Handbook of Adolescent Psychology,* 2nd edition, edited by Richard Lerner and Laurence Steinberg. New York: Wiley, 2011.

Kohlberg, Lawrence. *Essays on Moral Development:* Vol. 1, *The Philosophy of Moral Development.* San Francisco: Harper and Row, 1981.

Melton, Glennon. "This Is How to Win at Parenting and Life." *Huffington Post,* January 16, 2015. http://www.huffingtonpost.com/glennon-melton/this-is-how-to-win-at-parenting-and-life_b_6489048.html.

Merriam-Webster's Collegiate Dictionary, 11th ed., s.v. "love."

Petersen, Anne C. "Adolescent Development." *Annual Review of Psychology* 39 (1988): 583–607.

Rankin, Jane, David J. Lane, Frederick X. Gibbons, and Meg Gerrard. "Adolescent Self-Consciousness: Longitudinal Age Changes and Gender Differences in Two Cohorts." *Journal of Research on Adolescence, 14* (2004): 1–21.

Smahel, David, Bradford Brown, and Lucas Blinka. "Associations Between Online Friendship and Internet Addiction Among

Adolescents and Emerging Adults." *Developmental Psychology,* 48 (2012): 381–388.

Smetana, Judith. "Parenting Styles and Conceptions of Parental Authority During Adolescence." *Child Development* 66 (1995): 299–316.

Steinberg, Laurence. *Adolescence,* 10th edition. New York: McGraw Hill, 2014.

Sullivan, Harry S. *The Interpersonal Theory of Psychiatry.* New York: Norton, 1953.

Tanner, Daniel. *Secondary Education.* New York: Macmillan, 1972.

Wallis, Claudia. "What Makes Teens Tick?" *Time* magazine, *May 10,* 2004.

INDEX

Index

Index

ACKNOWLEDGMENTS

I would like to express my gratitude to the many people who took this journey with me. In writing this book, I leaned on many people. My sincere appreciation to all those who provided support, listened to my ideas again and again, offered fantastic feedback, patiently allowed me to vent and grumble, and assisted in proofreading, editing, and design.

To my loving and supportive parents, Manuel and Rosita Villanueva, whose unrelenting love and encouragement has never failed me. Thank you for keeping me grounded and teaching me what being a great parent is all about. Through your actions, guidance, and dedication, our family is strong, and we all thank you.

And finally, to my beautiful children: Susan, Thomas, Sophia, and Gabriel. You fill me with hope, and motivate me to do great things for you. I love you to the moon, stars, rocketships, rainbows...and all the way back.

ABOUT THE AUTHOR

Sara Villanueva, PhD, is an associate professor of psychology in Austin, Texas. She received her BA in psychology from the University of Texas at Austin, and her MS and PhD in developmental psychology from the University of Florida in Gainesville. Her area of specialization is adolescent development, with a specific focus on parent–adolescent relationships and parenting from various cultural perspectives. She teaches a range of courses such as Adolescent Psychology, Child Development, Cross-Cultural Lifespan Development, Developmental Psychopathology, and Human Sexuality. She also conducts research and has studied teens and their families for years.

Dr. Villanueva has published many articles and given a significant number of presentations to both academic and professional organizations around the globe. She is a teacher, researcher, author, and community leader. She is also the proud mother of four children: Susan, age 27, Thomas, 19, Sophia, 17, and Gabriel, 7. In addition to her formal training, Dr. Villanueva has several years of firsthand experience with raising teenagers under her belt, and is looking forward to the teen years with her youngest son. Being a single mother of four, she is well aware of the challenges that come with various family dynamics such as raising teens, single-parenthood, divorce and the impact on children, and blended-families: successes and failures, for example. Dr. Villanueva is clearly passionate about parenting adolescents and thrives by helping people to understand this tricky developmental period. She is a highly effective speaker who connects with people world-wide by sharing her expertise and unique experiences regarding adolescence and parenting, while also finding common ground with parents all over the world.